GLOVES

GLOVES

An Intimate History

ANNE GREEN

REAKTION BOOKS

Published by Reaktion Books Ltd
Unit 32, Waterside
44–48 Wharf Road
London N1 7UX, UK
www.reaktionbooks.co.uk

First published 2021

Printed and bound in India by Replika Press Pvt. Ltd

A catalogue record for this book is available from the British Library

ISBN 978 1 78914 458 1

Contents

Red silk glove decorated with pearls, jewels, enamel plaques and gold thread. The glove and its pair were made before 1220, probably in Sicily, and form part of the regalia of the Holy Roman Empire.

INTRODUCTION

Gloves have become the latest hue and cry of the style hounds.[1]

Gloves are the next big thing.[2]

Always wear gloves![3]

Declarations such as these from fashion journalists and glove manufacturers suggest that something exciting is happening to hand-coverings. 'The days of traditional utilitarian gloves in black and brown to keep out the cold are long gone,' says a representative of the Millau luxury glove company Causse. 'Our philosophy is to create gloves that are worn like jewels.'[4] Gloves in brilliant colours and dazzling designs are indeed increasingly in evidence, and practicality is hardly the point of the flamboyant versions regularly shown on the catwalk or in the pages of glossy magazines. There is justification for the excited headline 'The Glove Makes a Comeback'.[5]

Gloves have never really gone away, however. Over the centuries they have been assigned many different roles, and have assumed new and often contradictory meanings as patterns of fantasy and belief developed around them. Honour, identity, status and power have all been associated with gloves, as have decadence and deceit. They have been credited with magic powers, both good and evil. They have been treated as sexual symbols and have roles in courtship and marriage. The very act of glove-wearing, sometimes forbidden, sometimes mandatory, has attracted fierce responses ranging from moral outrage to aspiration and envy.

A tale from the French Renaissance exemplifies many of these attributes. An extraordinary glove is central to one of the narratives in *The Heptameron*, a collection of short stories first published in 1558. The glove is a small, lady's glove fastened with hooks of gold; its slim fingers are encrusted with diamonds, rubies, emeralds and pearls, and it is worn by an English lord, pinned to his cloak. The Englishman proudly explains the glove's origins to an intrigued French ambassador, telling him that it once belonged to a lady whom he had adored for seven years without ever daring to declare his love. On meeting her unexpectedly one day, he had been so overcome with emotion that he fell in a faint at her feet, and when the concerned lady offered help, he begged her to place her hand over his racing heart. She did so, but when he pressed her hand to his chest and began to declare his passion, she pulled away in alarm, leaving only the empty glove in his grasp. 'I have adorned it with the richest rings in my possession, though the riches I receive from the glove itself I would not exchange for the crown of England,' he tells the ambassador. 'There is nothing in the world more precious to me than to feel it as it presses against my side.' Although the Frenchman solemnly assures the English lord that his glove story proves him to be the truest lover that ever lived, he is secretly scornful, thinking that it would have been better to have won the lady's hand.[6]

Eye-catchingly ornate, the glove worn by the English lord is an object of display, and like many of the gloves discussed in this book, its opulence is indicative of wealth and social status. Like many of them, too, it is heavy with symbolism. Here it represents the absent woman whose hand it once adorned, and for the Englishman it is also an emblem of his undying love for her, and he wears it over his heart. However, gloves are flexible: they

In the presence of Richard II (1367–1400) and his court, Earl Marshal Thomas de Mowbray throws down a glove to challenge the Duke of Derby (later Henry IV) to a duel in this 15th-century manuscript. 'To throw down the gauntlet' has become a common idiom.

can be turned inside out, both literally and figuratively. So, while the Englishman considers the bejewelled glove to be the embodiment of pure passion, to the Frenchman it suggests the opposite. To him the empty glove signifies the lady's absence and the failure of the timid Englishman to win her heart and hand. Her glove may be a cherished memento and an emblem of love, but since it was neither honourably won nor freely given, it also invites contempt for its new owner. As this tale demonstrates, gloves can assume different and often contradictory meanings.

While many of the gloves discussed in this book are real, quite a few, like the glove in this tale, are fictional. Like its author, Marguerite de Navarre, writers and painters often include gloves in their work, recognizing how much significance can be subtly conveyed by a hand-covering. Revealing or concealing flesh, mediating contact, layering skin upon skin, easily reversible and sometimes barely distinguishable from the hand itself, gloves are as malleable and enigmatic as the messages they send out.

Just how deeply embedded in our culture they have become is evident from the way they have seeped into everyday language. We 'throw down the gauntlet' (or take it up) to issue (or accept) a challenge; we know that a 'velvet glove' may hide an iron fist; we 'handle someone with kid gloves' when we treat them gently, but when we are ruthless, 'the gloves are off'. Accomplices go 'hand in glove'. Garments 'fit like a glove'. Gloves' linguistic infiltration is not limited to the English language: a Frenchman 'turns someone inside out like a glove' if he makes them change their mind, and if he takes false credit for something, he is said to 'give himself gloves'.

From hand-knitted woollen mittens to exquisitely embroidered, sequined and beribboned confections, from sturdy working gloves to those so fine that a pair will fit into a walnut shell, from the three-fingered gloves of medieval shepherds to Bluetooth-enabled gloves that function like a mobile phone, gloves' extraordinary variety is a tribute to human ingenuity, as is the remarkable diversity of their cultural associations. The dictionary may define a glove as 'a piece of clothing that is worn on the hand and wrist for warmth or protection, with separate parts for each finger', but as this book aims to show, gloves are very much more than that.[7]

Mittens of crimson silk velvet and white satin, embroidered in England around 1600 with coloured silks and silver and silver-gilt thread. They are said to have been a gift from Elizabeth I to Margaret Edgcumbe, one of her maids of honour.

ONE

'Musk-scented, fragrant, invented by Venus': Early Gloves

Gloves' origins are lost in the mists of time. Humans have probably always used some form of covering to protect their hands from injury, for even orangutans in the wild have been seen wrapping leaves round their hands to avoid being hurt by prickly fruits or thorns. Some similarly primitive form of hand-wrapping was no doubt the distant ancestor of the glove.

Although Jean Godard, the French author of *Le Gan*, a long sixteenth-century poem in praise of gloves, says they came into being because hands needed protection from spines, he gives the hand-covering an exalted origin. In his fanciful account, he imagines the goddess Venus wanting to protect her hands from spiky plants and asking the Three Graces to cut and sew pieces of leather in the shape of her hands, 'to imprison them'. Their task accomplished, the Graces – personifying beauty, charm and elegance – also take to wearing gloves. From them the fashion spreads to royalty and the court, and eventually becomes universal, by which time gloves have developed other functions and forms:

> Protecting hands from heat, cold and dirt,
> Ring-bearing, plain, or richly trimmed,
> Musk-scented, fragrant, invented by Venus.[1]

The earliest references to gloves are to purely functional items rather than the perfumed luxuries of Godard's poem, and focus less on protection from injury than on keeping the hands warm. These early accounts do not always share Godard's enthusiasm. In the fourth century BC, the Greek historian Xenophon deplored the fact that the Persians had taken to wearing 'gloves for their hands and fingers' in winter; to him this was evidence of Persia's enfeeblement, showing how far the nation had degenerated since the glory days of Cyrus the Great.[2] Three centuries later, the Stoic philosopher Musonius Rufus was equally judgmental: he strongly disapproved of anyone 'soften[ing] the hands . . . by close-fitting gloves . . . unless perhaps in case of illness'.[3] Pliny, on the other hand, wrote approvingly about how the scribe of his uncle, Pliny the Elder, wore 'a particular sort of warm glove' so that cold weather would not interrupt their work.[4] Even in this early period, however, gloves had other, sometimes surprising functions. The Greek writer Athenaeus tells of a glutton who always wore gloves to the table so that he could grab pieces of meat while they were still too hot for his fellow guests to touch, and of a baker who wore gloves when kneading dough to prevent his perspiring hands from contaminating the cakes he was preparing for his wealthy employer.[5]

Judging by the curses invoked against glove thieves, gloves were highly prized possessions. When Docimedis, a Roman Briton living in Bath around the third century AD, discovered that someone had stolen his pair, he inscribed a curse tablet in the city's temple of Sulis Minerva with a plea for divine retribution: 'Docimedis has lost two gloves. He asks that the person who stole them lose his mind and his eyes in the temple where she appoints.'[6] Another curse tablet from the same period makes an equally impassioned plea to Mercury, asking the god to deprive a glove thief of 'blood and health'.[7]

We cannot know what those stolen gloves were used for, but many early forms of glove served to protect the hand from assaults more serious than anything that cold or thorns could inflict. An ultra-protective capacity was essential for gloves used in combat, and Greek and Roman artworks depict gloves designed not only to protect the hand but to intensify its physical force. The ancient Greeks developed a fighting glove that left the fingertips free but incorporated a sharp-edged leather knuckle-duster that greatly increased the power of a punch. Made of leather strips, such gloves covered the lower arm and ended in a fur cuff for wiping away the blood and sweat of the fight, as can clearly be seen in *Boxer at Rest*, the famous Hellenistic bronze sculpture from 100–50 BC. In Imperial Rome, similar gloves – *caesti* – were worn for combat, with spikes or jagged metal plates inserted to magnify the damage a hand could inflict. In his epic poem *The Aeneid* (written in around 30–19 BC), Virgil tells how the mere sight of such fearsome gloves, still 'stained with blood and spattered brains' after being used by the famous warrior Eryx, was enough to intimidate Dares as he and Entellus prepared to fight:

The hands of the bronze sculpture *Boxer at Rest*, 100–50 BC. The boxer wears fighting gloves that incorporate sharp-edged knuckledusters and fur cuffs for wiping away blood and sweat.

[Entellus] flung down a pair of gloves of giant weight, with whose hard hide bound about his wrists valiant Eryx was wont to come to battle. They stood amazed; so stiff and grim lay the vast sevenfold oxhide sewed in with lead and iron. Dares most of all shrinks far back in horror.[8]

Like the fighting gloves of Entellus, many medieval gauntlets (so named from the French 'gantelet', or 'little glove', though gauntlets were never diminutive) not only shielded the hand and wrist but transformed the hand into a weapon. Like *caesti*, some incorporated sharp metal protuberances to serve as knuckledusters. Others, often called 'forbidden gauntlets' because they were considered to give an unfair advantage at tournaments, had metal fingers that locked round a weapon to prevent it from being knocked out of the wearer's hand. Some, made of close-knit links of iron and lined with soft leather, followed the shape of the hand while preventing it from being slashed by an adversary's sword – not unlike modern stainless-steel mesh counterparts designed to protect a butcher's hands from the blade of a misjudged meat cleaver. Some gauntlets consisted of an armadillo-like carapace of overlapping metal plates that covered hand and wrist. Others had indentations at the end of each metal finger to represent fingernails, blurring the distinction between hand and glove and suggesting the uncanny presence of a superhuman hand of steel.

Gauntlets such as these did more than threaten adversaries or protect their owners' hands from injury. Many of the examples now preserved in museums are intricately ornamented, their elaborately etched and gilded patterns designed to show off the owner's wealth and social rank more clearly than a naked hand ever could. One particularly fine pair, thought to have been made for a son of Philip III of Spain and now in London's Victoria and Albert Museum, is lined with crimson velvet and features a

Steel gauntlets richly damascened in gold and silver with images of military trophies, palms and wreaths. They are thought to have been made in Spain around 1614 for a son of Philip III, and were intended for show rather than combat.

sophisticated pattern of palms, wreaths and military trophies, damascened in silver and gold. These gauntlets were meant not for battle but to be worn as an unambiguous declaration of status, wealth and military strength.

So powerful was the association between gloves and the social standing of their owner that even after death gloves remained a visible reminder of the status of the deceased. We see this in Geoffrey Chaucer's *Canterbury Tales*, where in 'The Knight's Tale' a grieving Theseus prepares Arcite's body for the funeral pyre and creates a rich spectacle of nobility that includes the dead knight's gloves:

> Theseus appointed one
> To fetch a bier and had it fitly clad
> In cloth-of-gold, the finest that he had.
> And in the self-same cloth he clad Arcite
> And on his hands white gauntlets, as was meet,
> He placed, and on his head a laurel crown
> And in his hand the sword of his renown.[9]

As emblems of his status a knight's gauntlets were often carried in his funeral procession and suspended above his burial place. The doeskin-lined copper-gilt gauntlets of the Black Prince, the eldest son of Edward III, remained hanging above his tomb in Canterbury Cathedral for centuries before being replaced by modern replicas; the originals, now fragile but still considered representative of the royal prince, are preserved under glass.

Gloves' ability to project status seems to have been recognized from earliest times. The oldest known surviving gloves were found among Tutankhamun's grave goods when his pyramid tomb was opened in 1920. Evidently selected to accompany the pharaoh on his journey into the afterlife, they had lain untouched since his death in 1323 BC, and included a small child's linen glove as well as several adults' gloves of varying lengths, among them a delicate, finely stitched pair made of red-and-blue-patterned tapestry. Too flimsy to offer the hand much protection, and unnecessary for warmth in the hot climate, their sole function was to display rank and prestige in this world and the next.

It is, of course, mostly the gloves of the elite that have endured. Gloves that once protected hands from manual labour have survived less well than those that drew attention to high

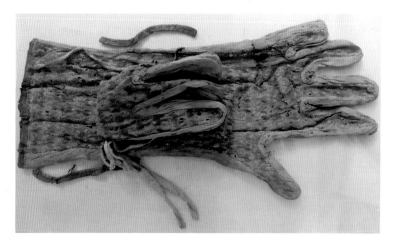

Red-and-blue-patterned gloves from the tomb of the Egyptian pharaoh Tutankhamun. They were buried with him in 1323 BC, and are the earliest known gloves in existence.

status. Although archaeologists have found a few simple woollen mittens in northern Europe dating from as early as the eighth
or ninth centuries, and although the Museum of London pre-
serves a late medieval labourer's battered leather mitten with a
tear that had been carefully mended to prolong its life, work-
aday gloves are likely to have been worn out and then discarded.[10]
Yet Godard's sixteenth-century poem celebrates the ordinary,
functional glove as well as its 'richly trimmed, musk-scented'
counterparts. On icy winter days, he points out, all essential
work would have to stop if there were no gloves; ploughing,
fishing and tending vines would be impossible if workers' hands
were not 'armed with good, thick, lined gloves of smoky hue'.[11]
He praises them for their functionality:

> I sing of [the hand's] forked gloves, which protect it
> From the heat of summer and the numbing cold
> Of icy winter. They also excel at
> Keeping it safe from harm, since all our wellbeing
> Depends on it alone: the practical glove
> Thus safeguards the careful, clever hand.[12]

Godard's poem is unusual in its appreciation of the everyday
glove, however. With a few exceptions, such as the three-fingered
pairs sometimes depicted on the hands of shepherds in medieval
illuminations, the gloves that feature in works of art and literature before the modern period are those of the wealthy.

As sartorial markers of a leisured class, such gloves convey
the message that the hands they enclose have never known manual labour. In *The Romance of the Rose*, a thirteenth-century
French allegory of courtly love, the figure of Idleness is char-
acterized, appropriately, by her pure white gloves and pure white
hands: 'There was never a girl more elegant or better arrayed . . .
she had white gloves to keep her white hands from turning
brown.'[13] The hands of the affluent drew attention to themselves

Early
16th-century
misericord
carving in the
form of a pair
of three-fingered
gloves, from
the church
of St Etienne
in Moudon,
Switzerland.
Similar gloves
appear in
medieval
depictions
of shepherds.

and their privileged status with gloves of increasingly elaborate decoration, richly embroidered with gold or silver thread, trimmed with ribbons or silken fringes, spangled with sequins or seed pearls, or – like the jewelled glove in the *Heptameron* tale mentioned in the Introduction – studded with precious gems. Fashionable gloves in early seventeenth-century England had exaggeratedly elongated fingers, stuffed at the tips, which not only suggested that an elegantly long-fingered hand lay within, but showed that that hand never needed to undertake practical tasks.

Royal gloves were particularly richly decorated. A monarch's glove was more than simply a visible sign of wealth and status, however. It was also a powerful symbol of royal authority, an authority it could embody even when far from the monarch's hand. An emissary carrying the king's glove was recognized as

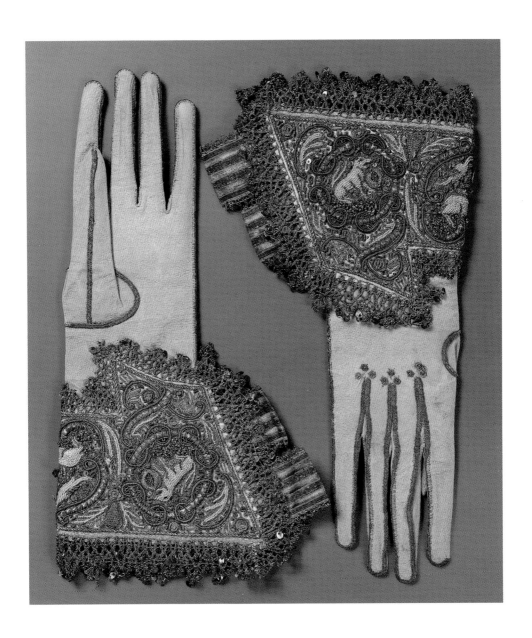

Early 17th-century English leather gloves, embroidered with seed pearls and several types of metal thread in a design of dogs, birds and deer, and trimmed with gold and silver bobbin lace and silk and metallic ribbon.

having been empowered to conduct royal business and had to be treated with due respect. Such was that sense of transferred authority that a large glove displayed at the entrance to a fair indicated that the event had royal permission.[14]

A glove's ability to convey the authority of a king has made its way into many works of fiction. One of the fourteenth-century tales in Giovanni Boccaccio's *Decameron* tells how the king of Sicily sent his glove to the king of Tunis as a royal guarantee of safe passage for a ship carrying the latter's daughter. When the ship is attacked by the Sicilian king's own grandson and heir, its crew produce the royal glove and claim immunity, but the Sicilian prince ignores the pledge and tries to abduct the princess. Rather than allow her to be taken by the Sicilian, the ship's crew preserve her honour by killing her. Such is the force of the glove-guarantee that the king of Sicily orders his grandson's execution, choosing to sacrifice his own heir rather than be known as a monarch who failed to honour the promise embodied by his glove.

In the eleventh-century French epic poem *La Chanson de Roland* (The Song of Roland), a glove serves not only as a symbol of royal authority but as a narrative device, reappearing at key points to underscore the poem's meaning. When several of Emperor Charlemagne's nobles offer to undertake a dangerous mission for him and ask for his glove and staff as proof that they come on behalf of their monarch, Charlemagne refuses their offers and instead chooses the reluctant Ganelon as his emissary. But the transfer of the imperial glove to Ganelon is bungled; the symbolism of the mishap warns the courtiers and the reader to expect Ganelon's future treachery and the French army's eventual defeat:

> The emperor offers him his right-hand glove,
> Yet Count Ganelon would rather have been elsewhere:
> As he was about to take it, he dropped it on the ground.

The French say: 'Good Lord, what can this mean?
From this embassy we shall suffer great losses.'
'My lords,' said Ganelon, 'you will hear more of this.'[15]

This is the first of several moments in the poem when a glove is passed from one person to another, but the transfer rarely goes smoothly, echoing the French and Saracen armies' long struggle for supremacy. The gloves are full of symbolism. They carry ominous undertones, underline the futility of human intentions and are never seen on a human hand. When the powerful emir Baligant gives a messenger a 'folded glove decorated with gold' to take to King Marsilie with an assurance that Baligant will help him fight the French, he instructs the messenger to make sure that Marsilie puts the glove on his right hand, unaware that Marsilie no longer has a right hand on which to wear it – his hand has been severed in battle.[16] Later, the dying Marsilie takes one of his gloves in his remaining hand and presents it to Baligant, saying:

I hereby hand over to you the whole of Spain,
And Saragossa and all dependent territory.[17]

But a left-hand glove transferred by a left hand does not augur well. After accepting the symbolic glove and the lands it denotes, Baligant is killed in battle before he can assume the dominion the glove apparently bestowed. Only when Roland, Charlemagne's beloved nephew, lies dying is there a successful transfer of a glove, but this time it is no human exchange. As an act of penance and in recognition that supreme power lies with God alone, Roland offers up his glove to heaven, and the Archangel Gabriel accepts from Roland's hand as angels descend to meet him.

If gloves carry such symbolic weight in this medieval epic, in the real world their symbolism could be equally powerful.

The dying
Roland offers
up his glove to
heaven in an early
14th-century
illumination.

In fifteenth-century Italy the Duke of Milan challenged the
Venetians to fight by sending them a bloodied gauntlet, a challenge which they accepted by returning two gauntlets dipped
in blood as a sign of good faith. However, when the Venetians
failed to engage in battle at the agreed time and place, the Duke
of Milan had their gauntlets hung up in public as battle trophies, to signal his claim of victory and the Venetians' shameful

failure to keep their word.[18] Heavily imbued with meaning, gloves served as visible statements of power and principle.

Nowhere, however, are their symbolic associations with status, honour and authority more evident than in their ritual role at coronation ceremonies. When medieval kings of France were crowned in Rheims Cathedral, their white gloves were anointed with holy oil and blessed, but after the ceremony the gloves were burned and their ashes scattered so that no one else might wear them and acquire the power believed to attach to them.[19] In England, in an ancient tradition that was still in force at the coronation of George IV in 1821, a member of the nobility, designated the King's Champion, would throw a steel gauntlet on the ground three times, and loudly defy anyone to challenge the rightful authority of the new monarch.[20]

Even today, a glove plays a significant role at British coronations. An embroidered white kid glove is presented to the monarch during the ceremony in a ritual that has been in place since 1377. A legal document from that year shows members of the nobility jockeying for position before the coronation of the ten-year-old Richard II, and records one ambitious gentleman's successful petition for the right to present the symbolic glove:

> William Furnivall, tenant of the manor of Farnham
> with the hamlet of Cere. Petition to find a glove for
> the king's right hand, and support the king's right arm
> so long as he should hold the rod. Claim admitted,
> the said William first taking the order of knighthood,
> which he did at Kennington on Tuesday before the
> coronation. Service performed.[21]

Unlike the iron fist implied by the steel coronation gauntlet thrown down in challenge, the soft white glove that covers the hand holding the sceptre is said to symbolize the gentleness and mercy with which the new monarch will reign. According to

Thomas Fuller, writing in 1655, the whiteness of the coronation glove is a visual emblem of purity and integrity and a reminder of the virtues of the saintly Edward the Confessor, so that 'when putting on the Gloves of this Confessour, [the monarch's] Hands ought to be like his, in moderate taking of Taxes from their Subjects.'[22]

For St Birgitta, the fourteenth-century patron saint of Sweden, gloves had a more complicated moral symbolism. Gloves, for her, formed a barrier between the hands within and the world beyond, and she viewed them as a graphic, if ambiguous, metaphor for the state of her soul. Although the comforting warmth of her thick gloves symbolized God's mercy, those gloves also conveyed her hopelessness and encouraged her to sin, for the manner in which she had pulled them on was defective. As she explained in her *Revelations*:

The gloves on my hands stand for the empty hope
I held. I thrust my works – symbolised by the hands
– into the large and thick mercy of God – denoted
by the gloves – but in such a way as not to feel
or notice God's justice when I touched it. Thus,
I became reckless in sinning.[23]

The coronation glove worn by Queen Elizabeth II at the ceremony in Westminster Abbey on 2 June 1953. For centuries, gloves have had an important symbolic role in coronation ceremonies.

Although the Catholic Church recognized that gloves could convey spiritual meaning, it was ambivalent about their ethical standing. Until the sixth century monks were forbidden by the pope to wear gloves when working in the fields, but later they were allowed utilitarian gloves – linen or canvas in summer, fur-lined in winter – for agricultural work, although they were to remove them for prayer or study.[24] Glove ownership was one of the prohibitions listed in the *Ancrene Wisse*, a thirteenth-century manual of advice for anchoresses.[25] But the Church soon came to appreciate gloves' richly symbolic potential and realized that control of ecclesiastical glove-wearing could be a means of marking clerical hierarchy and imposing discipline. Amid claims that the Apostles themselves had prescribed the wearing of gloves, the medieval Church developed a set of rules and conventions about which clerics might wear them, and in what circumstances. Distinctions were made between the gloves

Ecclesiastical gloves made for a bishop, knitted in red and yellow silk and embellished with silver-gilt bobbin lace. Spain, 16th century. Gloves have played an important role in Church liturgy since the Middle Ages.

of ordinary priests, the liturgical gloves of bishops, and gloves granted by the pope to high-ranking prelates, whereas glove-wearing by acolytes and other church helpers was strictly forbidden.[26]

In 1100 the Council of Poitiers had ruled that abbots should remain barehanded unless they or their order had been granted a papal privilege for the *usus chirothecarum* (the right to wear gloves), and when the lay sister Zwedera van Runen donned white gloves to read the holy scriptures in a fourteenth-century religious community in what is now the Netherlands, she was rebuked and told that such ostentatious cleanliness would condemn her to purgatory.[27] Bishops, however, were presented with white gloves, denoting purity, at their investiture, and in England it was customary for them to present a pair of gloves to all the guests at their consecration dinner. By 1678 that practice had become so expensive that it was banned and replaced by a £50 contribution towards the rebuilding of St Paul's Cathedral.

Commenting that gloves 'act as a sign of the great dignity of reverend prelates', Godard devoted a section of his poem to the distinctions between different glove-wearing clergymen, from wearers of the plainest to the most jewel-encrusted:

Each one of them wears [gloves]
That are made of wool, but of various types
Since they are not all as one; depending on their rank
Some have red [gloves] and others white.
In other cases the wool is covered with turquoises,
    rubies and green emeralds,
Which prelates wear as a mark of their honour
In being the lieutenants of our Sovereign Lord.[28]

Ecclesiastical gloves signified more than a churchman's status within the ranks of the clergy, however. Donning or removing them became a way of marking different stages in the ritual of the mass. Before putting them on, the celebrant said a special Latin prayer which alluded to the biblical account of Jacob covering his hands with goatskin, and implied that the gloves would purify the priest's hands and soul:

> O Lord, enclose my hands in the purity of a new man
> descended from heaven: just as Jacob, your chosen one,
> having concealed his hands with the skins of young
> goats, and having offered pleasing food and drink to
> his father, obtained paternal blessing, so too may I,
> having offered beneficial sacrifice by our hands, earn
> the blessing of your grace.[29]

But the celebrant removed his gloves before consecrating the bread and wine, and went similarly bare-handed when officiating at funerals or celebrating Good Friday mass, all moments of particular solemnity.

Liturgical gloves took on additional symbolism as they came to assume a sacred quality of their own. They were never made of leather, whose fleshly origins were considered too carnal for their spiritual role. Instead, in imitation of the seamless robe of Christ, they were knitted in a single piece, in wool or silk, and were worn in different colours according to the liturgical calendar. Their spiritual status was displayed to the congregation, for they were often decorated with embroidery representing the Christogram, or with enamelled metal discs depicting saints.[30] Some, such as the episcopal gloves preserved in the cathedral of Canosa in Italy, were constructed with normal thumbs but very short fingers in order to restrict the hands' movement and emphasize their ceremonial function.[31]

If the priest's hand was felt to be sanctified through contact with the special glove, in other cases this transfer of sanctity was reversed. Gloves could assume a mysterious power of their own, seemingly derived from the holiness of the hands that once wore

A 15th-century lead alloy pilgrim's badge representing the gloves of St Thomas à Becket. The glove pin indicated that the wearer had made a pilgrimage to the saint's shrine in Canterbury.

them. The gloves of the martyred St Thomas à Becket, for example, were said to have miraculously healed a nun, and medieval pilgrims wore metal badges in the shape of these gloves as a sign that they had visited the saint's shrine in Canterbury.

If power was felt to flow mysteriously between glove and hand, then depriving a man's hand of its glove could symbolize a removal of power. The ceremonial removal of gloves signalled that their wearer was divested of office – stripping him of his gloves was tantamount to stripping him of authority. So when Thomas Cranmer, Archbishop of Canterbury and a leader of the English Reformation, was convicted of treason and heresy in 1553, the ceremony of degradation to which he was subjected included the formal pulling off of his ecclesiastical gloves. Similarly, when one Sir Francis Michell was found guilty of criminal offences in 1621 and ceremonially stripped of his

knighthood, his gloves were removed and destroyed to demonstrate his definitive loss of status.[32]

The honesty and rectitude implicit in the biblical phrase
'clean hands and a pure heart' transferred from hands to gloves,
and gloves themselves became a metonym for integrity (Psalms
24:4). In *Love's Labour's Lost*, William Shakespeare – a glover's
son in whose plays gloves feature prominently – has Berowne
swear 'By this white glove' as a mark of his trustworthiness.[33]
Due to their association with honesty, gloves took on special significance in areas of the law and the administration of justice.
When a piece of land was sold, for example, the vendor, in the
presence of witnesses, would hand the purchaser a glove filled
with soil taken from the property as a guarantee of transfer of
ownership. Although the transaction was recorded in writing, in
the eyes of the law it was the transfer of the symbolic soil-filled
glove that constituted the contract. Similarly, a tenant would
confirm his tenancy by paying his lord in gloves.[34]

Records from as early as 1456 tell of pardoned criminals
presenting white gloves to a court of law to symbolize their innocence.[35] The English legal writer Ferdinand[o] Pulton (1536–1618)
was at pains to stress the probity of such gifts, insisting that they
followed an ancient precedent and were definitely not a bribe:

> If a man indicted and arraigned of Felonie, doth plead
> and shew forth the King's pardon of the same Felonie,
> which is allowed by the Court, whereupon hee doth
> pay and give his fees of gloves to the Justices, and
> other officers of the Court, this is no extortion, but
> an ancient fee, and lawfully done unto them.[36]

White gloves' association with innocence is also evident in
the old custom – which continued into the twentieth century –
whereby the sheriff would present a pair to the Assize Court
judge on the rare occasions when there were no cases for him

to try. It is seen, too, in the ancient practice of suspending a large white glove in a prominent place in town as a guarantee to criminals and debtors that they were immune from arrest during the local annual fair.[37] To this day, the eight-hundred-year-old Cherry Fayre in Axminster, Devon, opens with the ceremonial raising of a white glove and the traditional announcement: 'The Glove is up, the fayre's begin – let no man be arrested (or hung!) until the glove be down.'[38]

The role of gloves in legal matters did not always require them to be white. Sometimes it was simply intimate contact with their owners' hands that allowed gloves to act as proxies, representing the owner's case and guaranteeing his word. The official record of David Ramsey's trial for high treason in 1631 shows how solemnly their symbolism was treated. First the accuser, Lord Rea, threw down his red-brown glove 'for a Pawn or Pledge', then Ramsey threw down his white one. Both gloves were handed to the Lord Constable

> with due reverence; and the said Lord *Constable*,
> together with the Earl *Marshal*, committed them
> to the custody of the . . . Register of the Court.[39]

After both parties had presented their case and signed their written statements, the Lord Constable folded up Lord Rea's bill and placed it inside the red-brown glove, holding them in his right hand. Then, with Ramsey's white glove and written response in his left hand, he folded the two gloves and their contents together before decreeing that the matter was to be settled by a duel. In this legal dispute, the courtroom choreography of the gloves gave visual form to the fact that the judgement took the pleas of both parties equally into account.

However, like the garments themselves, the meanings of gloves could be turned inside out. They might stand for the trustworthy pledge of a handshake, but as items that covered and hid the hand, they could also be suspect, suggestive not of integrity but of concealment and deceit. If one strand of cultural reference links gloves to the honesty of their owner's hands, another inverts that association and views them as emblems of duplicity or fraud: dishonest hands or dishonest contents might lie beneath their innocent surface. Even in today's China, the white glove's traditional association with innocence and probity has been so thoroughly inverted that the term 'white gloves' is commonly applied to people suspected of money-laundering behind an apparently legitimate front.[40]

In the fifth-century BC the Greek historian Herodotus provided an early example of the distrust that hand-coverings have intermittently attracted down the centuries. He tells how Leotychidas, a corrupt ruler of Sparta, was caught red-handed when he was found to be sitting on a glove stuffed with bribes.[41] Sir Thomas More, as Henry VIII's Lord Chancellor, was well aware of gloves' suspect reputation, and when a Mrs Croaker presented him with a New Year's gift he was careful to avoid any suspicion of accepting a bribe. Grateful that her lawsuit had been successful, Mrs Croaker had given him a pair of gloves containing £40 in gold, but he returned the money immediately, explaining:

> It would be against good manners to forsake a gentlewoman's new-year's gift, and I therefore accept your *gloves* – their lining you will be pleased otherwise to bestow.[42]

Gloves have offered other grounds for suspicion. When perfumed gloves became fashionable in sixteenth- and seventeenth-century Europe, some suspected that their scent was a subtle way of administering poison, and poisoned gloves were blamed for several sudden deaths. Among the precautions against assassination that Lord Burghley drafted for Elizabeth I in 1560 was the careful inspection of 'Thyngs that shall touche any Part of your Majestie's Body bare', and particularly of scented gloves. He warned that 'no manner of perfume, ether in Apparel or . . . Gloves or such lyke . . . be presented by any Stranger, or other Persone, but that the same be corrected by some other fume.'[43]

The most famous alleged victim of poisoned gloves, Jeanne d'Albret, Queen of Navarre, almost certainly died from natural causes, but when Christopher Marlowe staged her death in his 1593 play *The Massacre at Paris*, he left his audience in no doubt that gloves were to blame. The Duke of Guise asks an apothecary:

> Where are those perfumed gloves which I sent
> To be poysoned, hast thou done them? speake,
> Will every savour breed a pangue of death?

The apothecary assures him that 'he that smelles but to them, dyes.'[44] In Marlowe's play the queen expires as soon as she inhales the gloves' lethal scent.

For the most part, however, gloves played a benign role in social exchange, particularly when offered as gifts. In some cases a donation of gloves implied the hope of spiritual recompense, as when the warrior Byrhtnoth presented 'a pair of skilfully made gloves' to Ely Cathedral in 991, anticipating that he would soon be killed in battle and would need divine mercy. In others, the gift of gloves helped to foster social or political bonds. A 1590 miniature by Nicholas Hilliard shows Sir George Clifford, newly appointed as Elizabeth I's champion, proudly wearing the queen's glove pinned to his plumed hat in a public display of the royal favour bestowed on him. The glove has been folded to show off its ornate cuff and the crown embroidered on its fingers, and like the jewelled glove displayed by the English lord in *The Heptameron*, it is worn to be visible by all.

Expensive gloves were often among the gifts exchanged between European courts. In 1588 the Spanish ambassador to the Medici court presented the Grand Duke of Tuscany with a gold and silver intarsia writing desk filled with perfumed gloves and other Spanish items, and by the end of that century the bulk of New Year's Day gifts exchanged between the major courts of Europe consisted of elaborately embroidered leather gloves.[45] Such gift-giving said as much about the donor as the recipient, whose hands they might not fit, and who might never wear them – the richest gloves were purely decorative statements, intended to be carried or attached to a belt or hat rather than worn on the hands. When the Dutch Republic sent 'six pairs of gloves embroidered with birds and fruitages in gold thread and seed pearls' to the sultan of Turkey in 1613, the gift was partly a mark of gratitude for the treaty the two countries had signed the previous year, but more importantly, it allowed the Republic to display its finest merchandise to the Turks.[46]

While signalling the donor's status, these glove-offerings were designed to establish or cement a relationship – commercial, political or otherwise – with the recipient, or to curry favour with a powerful superior. When Elizabeth I and her retinue were due to visit the University of Cambridge in 1578, Lord Burghley advised the heads of the university that

> they would do well to provide for the Earl of Leicester, the Lord Chamberlain, and the Earl of Oxford, some gloves, with a few verses in a paper joined to them, proper to every of their degrees.[47]

On that occasion the queen herself was presented with a Greek Testament, some verses and an exquisite pair of perfumed gloves, decorated with gold and embroidery, which had cost the princely sum of 60 shillings – equivalent to several months' wages for a skilled craftsman. To the relief of those attending, the gloves found favour with the queen:

Nicholas Hilliard, *George Clifford, 3rd Earl of Cumberland, c.* 1590.
Clifford wears Elizabeth 1's glove pinned to his hat in a proud display
of the queen's favour.

In taking the book and the gloves, it fortuned that
the paper in which the gloves were folded to open;
and her Majestie behoulding the beautie of the said
gloves, as in great admiration, and in token of her
thankful acceptation of the same, held up one of hir
hands, and, smelling unto them, putt them half waie
upon hir hands.[48]

Glove-giving rituals were not only for royalty and the aristocracy, however. Presented to mark special occasions or at
significant points in the calendar, particularly at Easter, gloves
were rooted in social exchange at many levels. During the medieval period it was customary for students graduating from the
University of St Andrews to present a pair to their teachers,
and at Leiden University in 1627 a young lawyer, Carel Martens,

Men's leather
mourning gloves
with inserts of
black silk linen
lace on the palms,
1730–60.

distributed 114 pairs as gifts to professors and others to cele-
brate his promotion.[49] Christenings and weddings were also
marked by gifts of gloves, and mourning gloves were handed
out at funerals, often in great quantities.

The practice was particularly widespread in eighteenth-
century New England. There, gloves were sometimes sent out
as an invitation to a funeral, but were more usually distributed
to mourners when the procession was about to leave for the
burial ground. Dr Andrew Eliot, pastor of the New North
Church in Boston, kept a meticulous record, month by month,
of all the gloves he received between January 1748 and his death
more than thirty years later. The entries distinguish between
gloves presented at funerals and those given out at weddings
and christenings, and note how many were of kid, or of lambs-
wool, or were women's gloves intended for his wife. Over a
32-year period Dr Eliot appears to have received 2,940 pairs of
gloves at religious ceremonies. Most of them he sold, supplement-
ing his income by 'fourteen hundred and forty-one pounds,
eighteen shillings, and one penny, old tenor'.[50]

The scale of glove-giving at the large funeral services of New
England's elite was exceptional: more than a thousand pairs
might be distributed at a grand funeral, and at the grandest of
all, a ceremony organized by wealthy Boston merchant Peter
Faneuil in 1738 to honour his uncle, over 4,000 pairs were given
away.[51] The ever-increasing ostentation and expense attracted
criticism, and in 1742 Massachusetts banned the large-scale gift-
ing of funeral gloves, yet the practice continued almost unabated
for another thirty years.[52] In their study of these New England
funerals, Steven Bullock and Sheila McIntyre confirm that large-
scale glove-giving was not just a display of the donor's status,
but an important way of forming and cementing social bonds:

> Elites also used gloves to reach out to other people,
> invoking widely held ideals of mutual respect, honour,

and inclusion and proclaiming membership in
the community at a time when that connection
was becoming particularly problematic . . .
general glove-giving became a means of signalling
mutuality.[53]

The shameful fact that the city of New York issued a decree in
1748 prohibiting slaves from wearing gloves at funerals further proves this point, their gloveless hands signalling social
exclusion rather than mutuality.[54]

Whereas New England's relatively short-lived glove-
distribution rituals were regional and exceptional, Samuel
Pepys provides a more representative insight in the diaries that
he kept in the 1660s as he went about his everyday life in London.
The diaries are full of references to gloves, and show Pepys frequently buying them as gifts as well as for his own use; sometimes
he lingers in a glove shop for longer than necessary, buying a
pair as an excuse to spend time with a pretty shop-girl. His purchases often came from stores in Fenchurch Street or the New
Exchange, but on 25 January 1669 his wife was greatly tempted
by gloves from a different source. His friend Batelier had just
returned from France, bringing with him

a great many gloves perfumed, of several sorts; but all
too big by half for [my wife], and yet she will have two
or three dozen of them, which vexed me and made me
angry; so she at last, to please me, did come to take
what alone I thought fit; which pleased me.[55]

The diaries reveal how fully glove-giving had been absorbed
into rituals of social exchange by that time. Pepys wins 'a payre
of gloves of a Crowne' in a wager.[56] He witnesses ambassa-
dors from Russia presenting a hawking glove 'wrought with
gold' to the king.[57] Every spring he and his friends draw lots to

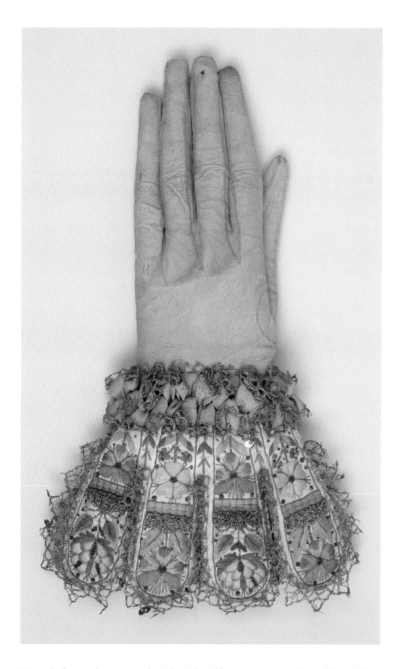

Man's kid gauntlet trimmed with pink ruffles, 1600–1620. The tabbed silk cuff, edged with gold lace and spangles, is embroidered with flowers, and the elongated fingers emphasize freedom from manual work. Elaborately embroidered gloves were favoured as New Year gifts in the major European courts of the time.

determine who is to be their Valentine, a status sealed by the gift of gloves. In February 1661 Pepys presents his Valentine for that year, Martha Batten, with 'a payre of embroydered and six payre of plain white gloves' costing 40 shillings, while his wife receives 'half-a-dozen pairs of gloves and a pair of silk stockings and garters' from Sir William Batten, Martha's father, who has drawn her name in the Valentine lottery.[58] Some years Pepys gives a dozen pairs to his Valentine, other years eight. Attending a wedding, he notes that 'I was well received and had two pair of gloves, as the rest'; at a christening, 'we had gloves and wine and wafers, very pretty.'[59] And on 2 February 1663 he discovers a most welcome surprise inside a pair of white gloves that he is given for his wife:

> Off to the Sun Taverne with Sir W. Warren, and with
> him discoursed long, and had good advice, and hints
> from him, and among other things he did give me a
> payre of gloves for my wife wrapt up in paper, which
> I would not open, feeling it hard; but did tell him that
> my wife should thank him, and so went on in discourse.
> When I came home, Lord! in what pain I was to get
> my wife out of the room without bidding her go, that
> I might see what these gloves were; and, by and by, she
> being gone, it proves a payre of white gloves for her and
> forty pieces in good gold, which did so cheer my heart,
> that I could eat no victuals almost for dinner for joy to
> think how God do bless us every day more and more.[60]

Although most of the pairs he buys are plain, Pepys is sensitive to the charms of pretty gloves. He spends 10 shillings at the New Exchange on 'pendents and painted leather-gloves, very pretty and all the mode'; he purchases jasmine-scented gloves for women friends; and on one occasion, in a particularly generous mood, he buys his wife 'a pair of gloves trimmed with yellow ribbon (to [match the] petticoat she bought yesterday), which cost me 20s'.[61] The price of gloves is important to him. Comparing his kid gloves with those of a friend, he is disconcerted to discover that although the friend's gloves are 'as handsome, as good in all points' as his own, they 'cost him but 12d a pair, and mine me 2s' – twice as much.[62] Their monetary value aside, however, gloves also mark the clinching of a deal. In early January 1669, a week after signing an agreement to pay his wife a generous annual allowance of £30, Pepys records receiving a reciprocal gift of gloves from her to seal the pact: 'my wife did give me my pair of gloves, which by contract she is to give me in her £30-a-year.'[63]

Gloves were so intimately woven into the fabric of Pepys's life that they seeped into his subconscious, and on at least one occasion they assumed strange new meanings as he slept. Shortly after the death of his mother in June 1667, he had disturbing dreams about her, which revolved around a pair of mourning gloves. In the dreams, he and his wife are leaving his office when they are met by his mother, father and sister:

> My mother told me she lacked a pair of gloves, and
> I remembered a pair of my wife's in my chamber and
> resolved she should have them. But then recollected how
> my mother came to be here when I was in mourning for
> her; and so thinking it to be a mistake in our thinking
> her all this while dead, I did contrive that it should be
> said to any that enquired, that it was my mother-in-law,
> my wife's mother, that was dead and we in mourning
> for. This dream troubled me and I waked.[64]

Outstripping even real gloves in the flexibility of their connotations, the dream gloves convey a confusion of etiquette anxiety, identity displacement and grief, as Pepys struggles to come to terms with his mother's death.

By that time gloves had acquired a vast array of social and cultural meanings in addition to their practical functions, and were widely worn. Earlier in the century Horatio Busino, chaplain to the Venetian ambassador to London, had been struck by how many people he saw wearing gloves in the capital. In July 1618 he had reported back to Italy that although there was great variation in Englishwomen's headgear and in the texture, cut and colour of their clothes, in one respect they all dressed alike: 'all wear very costly gloves. This fashion of gloves is so universal that even the porters wear them very ostentatiously.'[65] But if the fashion for gloves seemed to have reached a peak in the seventeenth century, it was to be far surpassed two centuries later, when glove-wearing and glove-making entered a remarkable new phase.

Sterling silver glove darner, one of many glove-related accessories produced in the 19th century.

TWO

Tranks, Forgits and Quirks: Making Gloves

T he nineteenth century saw an extraordinary transformation in the fortunes of gloves. There were radical changes in how they were made, how they were sold, how they were worn and how they were thought about, with major social consequences for the areas where they were manufactured. Until the 1830s the glove-making process had remained relatively unchanged for hundreds of years. Some gloves were hand-knitted, some were cut from fabric such as linen, but those preferred by the upper classes were usually made of fine leather. Unlike shoes, whose design made no distinction between the left and right foot before the late eighteenth century, leather gloves were differently shaped to fit left and right hands. They might vary in length and decoration according to fashion, but they continued to be produced according to centuries-old tradition: made individually, cut with shears from carefully prepared skins and hand-stitched with needle and thread.

As early as the tenth century, makers of leather gloves had begun to form themselves into associations. In Scotland, King William the Lion signed a charter in 1210 granting special privileges to the Perth glovers' guild, the first of several royal charters accorded to the town's glove trade. The Worshipful Company of Glovers of London was founded in 1349, and their status as craftsmen was confirmed in 1638 by a royal charter that allowed members to stamp out some of the abuses that had crept into the trade, granting them the right 'to search for, and destroy, bad

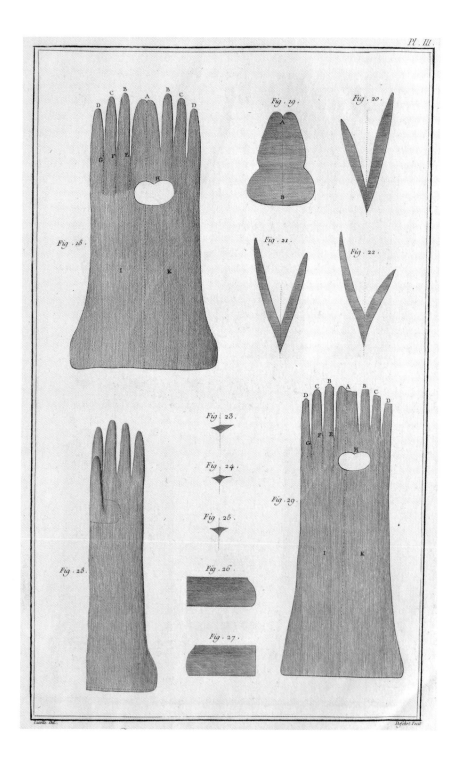

Illustrations from Diderot and D'Alembert's *Encyclopedie* of 1751, showing
glove-making tools and glove pieces.

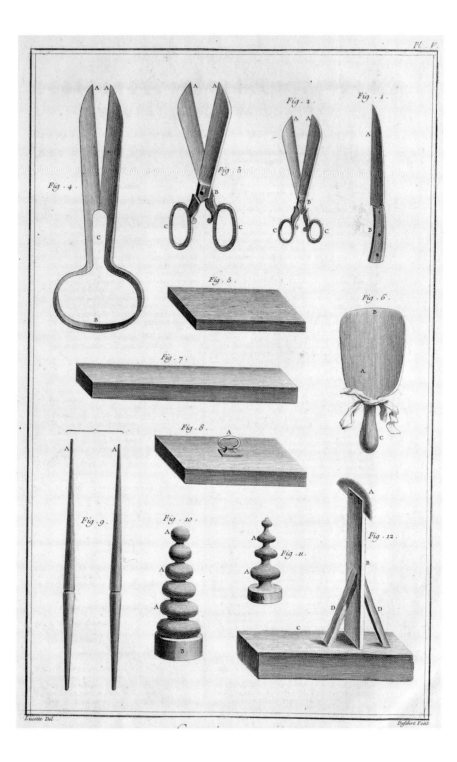

Pl. V.

Fig. 1.

Fig. 2.

Fig. 3.

Fig. 4.

Fig. 5.

Fig. 6.

Fig. 7.

Fig. 8.

Fig. 9.

Fig. 10.

Fig. 11.

Fig. 12.

or defective skins, leather, or gloves'.[1] The charter's forceful preamble paints a vivid picture of the shoddy workmanship produced by unskilled outsiders who took up unauthorized glove-making after moving to London:

> working of gloves in chambers and corners, and
> taking apprentices under them, many in number,
> as well women as men, that become burdensome to
> the parishes wherein they inhabit, and are a disordered
> multitude, living without proper government, and
> making *naughtie and deceitful gloves*.[2]

In France, too, glove-makers formed their own corporations and apprenticeship systems, and sought to maintain high standards. In 1290, for example, Parisian glovers were banned from working at night, a measure introduced to prevent the poor-quality work caused by poor light. The ruling meant that glove-makers were unable to work after 4 p.m. during winter and were faced with heavy fines if they failed to comply. Although the ban may have raised standards of workmanship, glove-makers complained that it deprived them of income and left their apprentices with time to indulge in 'gambling and all manner of dissolute behaviour'.[3] After objections that the regulation was not in the public interest, it was eventually modified in 1467 to allow glove-makers to work between five in the morning and ten at night.

The gloves they produced were of many different kinds, and cut from a wide variety of leathers. French medieval post-mortem inventories list gloves made from fine white lambskin, kid, cat, fox, chamois, deer and especially hare. (It should be noted, however, that glove leathers did not always come from the animal named. 'Dogskin', for example, might in some cases come from a dog, but it could also refer to dogfish skin, or to a similarly strong and flexible type of sheepskin.) Sometimes the inventoried gloves were plain; sometimes they were more elaborate, and lined with fabric or leather like the fine lambskin gloves that appear on one list, 'the one lined in dogskin, embroidered, the other lined in wolfskin, tanned and embroidered'.[4] Rarest and most highly prized were those made from the sheerest layer of skin, so fine that a pair could fit into a walnut shell; later these came to be known as Limericks, named after the Irish town that specialized in making them. Henry III of France and his court favourites are said to have worn such gloves overnight, impregnated with perfume and moisturizing unguents to soften and whiten their hands. By the end of the sixteenth century these expensive and delicate creations were so sought after that, rather than being worn on the hands, they were sometimes dangled ostentatiously from the waist.[5]

Such was the skill required to make good gloves that by the mid-seventeenth century a Parisian glove-maker had to spend four years as an apprentice, followed by three years as a working glover, before he could hope to earn the grade of Master.

Limerick gloves, made from the sheerest layer of skin, were so fine that a pair could fit inside a walnut shell.

To qualify as a Master he had to produce five types of glove to the highest standard: a five-fingered glove made of otter fur; a dogskin hawking glove; a scalloped glove, lined throughout; a lady's kid glove with finger slits for displaying jewelled rings; and a gentleman's cut-away sheepskin glove.[6] All had to be perfectly stitched, dyed and scented, for by this time glovers were also specialist perfumers; the fashion for perfumed gloves, said to have been introduced to the French court from Italy in the 1550s by Catherine de' Medici, had quickly spread across Europe among a social elite – both male and female – who could afford such luxuries.

In June 1562 Sir Nicholas Throckmorton, Elizabeth I's ambassador to Paris, wrote to his counterpart in Madrid asking him to send two pairs of gloves perfumed with orange flowers and jasmine, 'th' one for my wives hand, the other for myne owne'.[7] Throckmorton's request may appear to imply that the gloves would be lightly scented with a delicate floral fragrance, but contemporary accounts indicate that perfumed gloves – particularly those from Spain or treated 'in the Spanish style' – were usually so heavily scented that their smell could be overpowering. Fernando de Rojas's Spanish tragicomedy *Celestina* of 1499 describes how a room fills with the scent of oranges when a woman removes her gloves, and the French philosopher Michel de Montaigne said that if ever his gloves touched his bushy moustache, their perfume would linger on it for the rest of the day.[8]

The pungent fragrance of gloves helped to mask foul odours and the unpleasant smell of poorly prepared leather, but that was not its only usefulness. Perfume was thought to protect the wearer from epidemics at a time when bad air and offensive smells were believed to transmit disease. Fine perfumed gloves thus had therapeutic as well as aesthetic value, and even the intensely puritanical Oliver Cromwell is known to have owned scented versions.[9] As an extravagant fashion of the elite, however, they were often the butt of satire, as when the playwright

Ben Jonson mocked the greed and vanity of the aptly named Sir Epicure Mammon in his play *The Alchemist* by having him aspire to owning ludicrously rarefied

> gloves of fishes' and birds' skins, perfumed
> With gums of paradise and eastern air.[10]

As the fashion for scented gloves became increasingly widespread in the later sixteenth and seventeenth centuries, it was not only skilled professional glove-makers who undertook their perfuming. In *The English Huswife*, a book of recipes and remedies published in 1623, Gervase Markham wrote that the ability to perfume gloves was one of the '*inward and outward Vertues which ought to be in a compleate Woman*', and he offered his female readers detailed instructions on how to do it at home:

> *To perfume gloves.* Take Angelica-water and Rose-
> water, and put into them the powder of Cloves,
> Amber-greece, Muske and Lignum Aloes, Beniamine
> and Callamus Aramattecus; boyle these till halfe
> bee consumed; then straine it, and put your Gloves
> therein; then hang them in the Sunne to drie, and
> turne them often; and thus three times wet them,
> and drie them again: or otherwise take Rosewater
> and wet your Gloves therein, then hang them up
> till they be almost drie; then take halfe an ounce of
> Beniamine, and grind it with Oyle of Almons, and
> rub it on the Gloves till it be almost dried in: then
> take twentie grains of Amber-greece, and twentie
> grains of Muske, and grind them together with
> Oyle of Almons, and so rub it on the Gloves, and
> then hang them up to drie, or else let them drie in
> your bosome, and so after use them at your pleasure.[11]

Lucas Cranach the Elder, *Judith Victorious*, *c.* 1530. Judith wears gloves
with finger slits to display her rings.

Few professional glove-makers are likely to have dried their handiwork in their bosom, but Markham's recommendation to English housewives to do just that highlights the intimacy of gloves' relation to the body. Although the still-damp gloves are not yet ready to be worn, they are pressed against flesh, absorbing bodily warmth and mingling the scent of human skin with the carefully perfumed leather, as they will continue to do when worn on the hands. As Chapter Five shows, the intimate communion of glove and body has provided many writers with a usefully suggestive image.

Perfumed gloves are rarely produced today, but they are not quite extinct. The French parfumier Guerlain recently collaborated with luxury glove-makers Agnelle to produce a limited number of fine black lambskin gloves for men, lined in

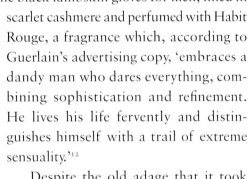

scarlet cashmere and perfumed with Habit Rouge, a fragrance which, according to Guerlain's advertising copy, 'embraces a dandy man who dares everything, combining sophistication and refinement. He lives his life fervently and distinguishes himself with a trail of extreme sensuality.'[12]

Despite the old adage that it took three nations to create the finest gloves – 'Spain to dress the leather, France to cut it and England to sew it' – glove-making flourished especially in regions with easy access to supplies of suitable leather, whether from kid, calf or lamb.[13] Between 1790 and 1820 nearly half of all British glovers were based in or around Worcester, an area known for sheep-rearing since medieval times, and where the earliest record of a glove-maker dates back to the

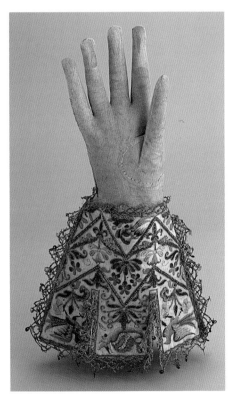

Man's castor (soft goatskin) gauntlet with elaborate tabbed satin cuff embroidered with flowers, scrolls and birds and edged in gilt lace. Gloves such as these were designed for courtly display. This pair was made in England *c.* 1625–50 for the first Lord Fairfax.

thirteenth century. In France, the towns of Millau and Grenoble became important glove-making centres for similar reasons, rivalling Paris and producing gloves to the highest standard. Grenoble was already well known for its leather gloves by the early fourteenth century, and its reputation was further enhanced when a prominent Grenoble glove-maker, Mathieu Robert, was appointed glover and perfumer to Henry IV in 1606.

Because of this distinction, rather more is known about Robert than about other glove-makers of the period. Like many of them, he came from a family whose members had been in the glove trade for generations, and the fact that he was made a municipal magistrate shows that he was highly respected in the community. The post-mortem inventory of his effects gives some indication of his business and demonstrates why his work found royal favour: on his death his workshop contained not only ingredients for perfuming gloves – musk, eau de Naples, rose-wood, sandalwood and fragrant powders – but 2,400 lambskin gloves, 1,400 kid gloves and 600 gloves made from other leath-ers, including chamois and goose. Many of these were clearly intended for wealthy aristocratic customers who could afford Robert's rich confections of blue, green or wine-coloured skin, trimmed with gold or silver lace and decorated with silk taffeta embroidered in gold thread, and for whom exquisitely crafted and scented hand coverings were not only a pleasure to possess but an important status symbol.[14]

Wearing conspicuously expensive gloves was unwise during the turbulent years of the French Revolution and its aftermath, however, when glove-making went into a steep decline in France. A fine yellow glove from that period, now in the Palais Galliera in Paris, shows how careful glove-wearers had to be in those dan-gerous and unstable times. Originally decorated with the royalist slogan 'Vive le roi' (Long live the king), this glove has had the wording inexpertly altered to 'Vive la loi' (Long live the law) in an attempt to signal anti-royalist fervour. Covering the hands was felt to be out of step with the new ideology's demands for openness and personal authenticity, and it was safer for an aristocrat to go bare-handed than to draw attention to his rank by displaying extravagantly ornate gloves.

In 1787, shortly before the Revolution, Grenoble's glove industry employed 6,254 people; twenty years later, that figure had fallen to around 2,800.[15] A shortage of fine glove leather exacerbated the slump in manufacturing, as did the trade embargoes of the Napoleonic wars, which prevented the export of gloves from France to Britain. But although they could no longer enter the country legally, fine French gloves were still much sought after by fashionable Englishwomen, and smugglers were quick to exploit lucrative opportunities, such as the sending of contraband gloves across the Channel concealed inside fishermen's boots or hollowed-out loaves of bread.[16]

The revolutionary period had repercussions for the glove industry in Britain as well as France. English glove-making benefited from the sudden reduction in French competition, and the industry grew, despite an attempt by the government of William Pitt the Younger to raise revenue by imposing a tax on gloves. A one-penny stamp duty was added to all gloves costing less than ten pence; twopence was added to gloves of between ten and fifteen pence; and threepence to all that cost more. Retailers who sold gloves without displaying the words 'Dealer in Gloves' on their shopfront faced heavy fines, as did anyone who bought or sold gloves without stamp duty. Pitt's opponent, Charles James Fox, was sceptical about the scheme, pointing to the large numbers of *'children, labourers and other inferior classes of mankind who never consumed this article'*, and indeed the unpopular glove tax raised only a small fraction of the revenue anticipated. After nine years, the government conceded failure and the Act was repealed in 1794.[17]

This was nevertheless a productive period for English glove-making. Worcester's output reached its peak between 1790 and

MORNING DRESS.   FULL DRESS.

Two Englishwomen, one in morning dress, the other in full dress, wearing the long, loose-fitting gloves fashionable in the early 19th century. Ladies Monthly Museum, London, 1 October 1804.

1820, with 150 manufacturers employing over 30,000 people in and around the town. Quality improved, too, due in part to the invention in 1807 by a Somerset man of the 'gloving donkey', a wooden stand with a toothed clamp that held the pieces of leather firmly together and helped to ensure even stitching. Although the device was introduced to France in 1816, it was not enough to restore that country's flagging glove production, but the situation soon reversed after Britain lifted its import ban in 1826. Fine French gloves poured across the Channel, causing British glove-makers to suffer in their turn. By 1829 the *Sherborne and Taunton Journal* was reporting the devastating effect of these imports on the local community:

The gloving donkey, invented by James Winter in 1807, had a toothed clamp to hold glove pieces in place. It allowed the sewer to work more quickly and stitch more evenly.

The situation of our neighbouring poor who used to find employment in the glove manufactory in the town of Yeovil and all the adjoining districts, is, we regret to say, very distressing; and when we look at the extent of the importation of foreign gloves, we see little prospect of any improvement. The quantity imported this year to the end of the month of April is 24,813 dozen, which would have given employment for 100 days to 1,000 women and children for the sewing, and a proportionate number of men and boys in the dressing and preparing the leather.[18]

In his 1834 *History of the Glove Trade*, William Hull, a Yeovil glover and fierce protectionist, deplored the fact that many London glove manufacturers, unable to compete with

French imports, had turned instead to selling French gloves that had often entered the country illegally. Anyone purchasing these foreign gloves showed a shameful lack of patriotism, he wrote:

> If a patriotic feeling were more generally evinced by the aristocracy or gentry, much of the evil arising from unwise laws and regulations would be averted.
>
> If the purchasers of French gloves would reflect that they were depriving the English artisan of the wages of making such gloves and calculate what must be the loss on the consumption of French gloves last year [1832] passed through the Custom-house – and which may be considered not much more than one-half the quantity brought into the country – they would hesitate before they gave to the foreigner that bread which they might, with so much consistency and justice, supply to their own ill-employed, and therefore naturally discontented, fellow-countrymen.[19]

The examples Hull quotes to demonstrate the sudden collapse of British glove-manufacturing and the resultant hardship are striking. Ludlow, where more than a thousand people – about a fifth of the town's population – had previously been employed in the glove trade, had only six men still working in gloving by 1832. The Leominster glove trade employed nine hundred people in 1825, but only 163 in 1831. In Ireland, where the situation was no better, a pair of exquisitely fine Limerick gloves had become 'almost as rare as a black swan'. Such was the importance of the glove industry that the widespread failure to buy home-produced gloves was, for Hull, not only 'lamentable proof of the decay of those feelings and principles, which formerly distinguished the English character', but a sign of impending national disaster.[20]

If the French glove industry benefited from the lifting of the trade ban in 1826, nearly a decade later it received an even more powerful impetus which not only triggered an astonishing recovery but was to change how leather gloves were manufactured at home and abroad. The transformation was largely due to Xavier Jouvin, the inventive son of a Grenoble glove-maker. After spending more than five years studying the different shapes and sizes of the hands of patients at the town's hospital, Jouvin devised a mathematical system of 320 glove sizes that could

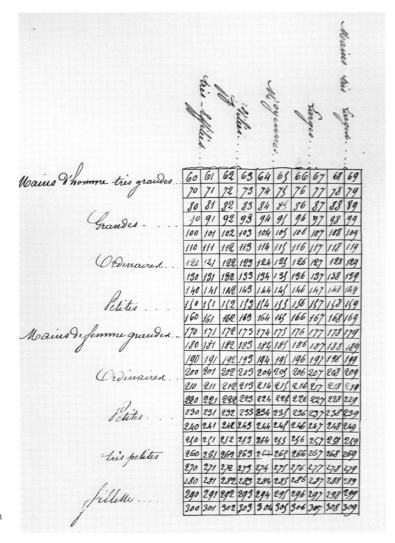

Xavier Jouvin's chart of glove sizes, devised to allow any hand to have a well-fitting glove. The sizes range from 'very large man with very broad hands' to 'young girl with very slim hands'.

guarantee a good fit for any hand. Before this, glove-fitting and even glove-pairing had been a time-consuming process of trial and error for customer and vendor, but Jouvin's procedure meant that correctly sized, perfectly paired gloves could be sold quickly and efficiently, and a variant of his system is still used today. Soon after perfecting his sizing system, Jouvin developed his *main de fer* (iron hand), a calibrated mechanical cutter that could punch out precisely measured glove pieces from multiple layers of skin at a time. He took out French patents on his inventions in 1834 and 1838, and Grenoble's glove industry prospered as well-fitting Jouvin gloves became increasingly sought after at home and abroad.[21] The expiry of these patents in 1849 caused a massive surge in France's production of leather gloves as other centres adopted the new technology: worth 20 million francs in 1847, national output had soared by 1851 to 47 million francs, making it one of France's most important industries.[22]

The huge expansion in glove manufacture had a significant effect on French life. It not only boosted the national economy, but had a substantial impact on animal rearing, since, on average, the skins of eight young goats were needed in order to produce a dozen kid gloves. The numbers involved are astounding. The *Bulletin de la société de statistique* for 1851 calculated

The *main de fer* (iron hand), a calibrated mechanical cutter patented by Xavier Jouvin, which could punch out precisely measured glove pieces from multiple layers of skin.

that Grenoble alone had needed 2,560,000 kidskins that year to create its *gants chevreau*, and the town had used 75,000 eggs a week to treat the fine glove leather, about three times as many as were consumed by the inhabitants.[23]

Production kept rising, but so did demand, for a rapidly growing middle class were coming to see gloves as an important emblem of their gentility. By 1867 France's leather glove industry employed 65,000–70,000 workers and produced about 2 million dozen pairs – an output of roughly 48 million leather gloves a year.[24] About three-quarters of these were exported, mainly to England, while most of England's own soaring glove output was exported to America. Demand for gloves seemed insatiable, and it soon became clear that only by adopting new manufacturing methods could producers meet a rapidly expanding international market.

More countries were starting to produce gloves, and foreign competition was fierce. A report for France's Ministry of Trade and Industry that looked back over developments in the nation's glove industry during the course of the nineteenth century outlined the changing international situation:

> At the end of the century, England was in more or
> less the same position as in 1889. Germany increased
> and improved its manufacturing, benefiting from the
> advantage of cheap labour. Major factories opened
> in the United States, to France's detriment. In Italy,
> Naples made progress thanks to the low wages of
> its artisans. Vienna and Prague are active producers.
> Two facts have dominated in recent years: a growth
> in consumption and a fall in price.[25]

The same report also described how international competition had spurred French glove-makers to modernize their industry:

Our competitors moved more quickly than we did
to transform their manufacturing processes. They
built enormous factories and introduced modern
improvements, applying division of labour and
bringing together leather preparation, dying, stitching
and embroidery. The situation [in France] became
critical, but today it is secure. Machinery has been
widely adopted by French manufacturers, who have
built large factories with machines powered by steam,
hydraulics or gas, and installed electric lighting in
place of gaslight, which affected the colours. They
have established agencies and outlets in the United
States, in South America, in England and in Australia.[26]

The new processes brought new efficiency, allowing a greater
variety of gloves to be produced, and so stimulating fashions
to change more rapidly. A column in the *Strawbridge and Clothier's Quarterly* of 1883 gives a taste of the profusion of styles
then on offer to American consumers as it tempts its readers to
choose from among the latest designs:

It will be good news to many to learn that the popular
Mousquetaire gloves can now be bought in silk, Lisle,
and cashmere. Gants de Suede are more favoured
for spring wear than kid. Gloves à la Gillette have
the wristlets formed of alternate stripes of kid and
insertion. Silk and tinsel embroidered gloves come
in for a share of admiration. The leading tints are,
terra-cotta, crushed strawberry, beige, olive, tan, puce,
ochre-yellow, dove-color, and silver gray. Both black
and white Mousquetaires, very long, are fashionable;
the former are worn with light costumes, the latter
with dark. Among the novelties . . . is a long glove with
the fingers cut half way off, called the dinner glove.[27]

GLOVES.

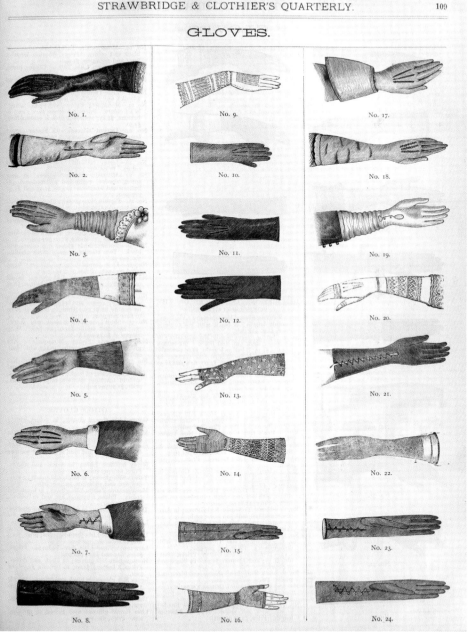

Page from the *Strawbridge and Clothier's Quarterly* showing
a range of the glove styles for sale in America in the 1880s.

With increased industrialization had come new glove-related inventions. In 1849 a French patent was granted to a M. Deraine for a machine that rapidly smoothed and folded gloves, allowing them to be neatly stacked and packaged by the dozen.[28] Since the glove's close fit and the position and shape of the thumb were of particular concern, inventors experimented with cutting machines that altered the position both of pieces and of seams in attempts to improve tightness without loss of flexibility. In 1853 a glove merchant named Maury developed a new kind of glove button that allowed the glove to be tightened without being stretched, and made it easier to remove; the introduction of dome fasteners, patented by Albert-Pierre Raymond in 1886, further simplified the process. Tight gloves necessitated glove-stretchers, which ranged from simple wooden devices to ornate implements of ivory or silver. There were machines for attaching buttons, for polishing and for finishing, as well as more fanciful creations, including an unlikely gadget patented by Ernest Wise and Walter Gardner, two London jewellers, in 1919: 'a combination brooch, cigarette holder and glove button-hook or nail-cleaner', which promised to 'save the smoker from staining the finger or the glove with the nicotine'.[29]

In the 1860s, however, the most important challenge for inventors was to devise a sewing machine suitable for leather gloves. This presented major difficulties, and although the Danish clockmaker Hans Peter Henriksen exhibited a machine at the 1867 Exposition universelle in Paris, it proved to be unsuitable for commercial use. By the 1878 exhibition, however, a number of new glove-stitching machines were on show, and one remained in operation throughout the exhibition so that a fascinated public could watch it function.

The official report from that exhibition reveals the extent to which French national pride and identity were bound up with glove-making. England, Belgium and Austria might produce good gloves, it conceded, but France reigned supreme:

Parisians are the finest artists in the world when it
comes to dressing humanity from head to toe. Look
at the glove industry. England is perhaps the country
that wears the most gloves on earth, for English
gentlemen use more of them than men from other
countries, and one of the privileges of the women
of every civilised nation is always to have their hands
covered with stitched sheepskin. England, where
consumption is high, manufactures gloves in great
numbers and does it well. England has fine leather,
solid and well dyed, and excels in double seaming,
which has made English gloves for travel and horse-
racing famous. Belgium is also making good progress;
its exhibit was charming. But if you confuse a Belgian,
English or Viennese glove with one from Paris or
Grenoble, you are unworthy of wearing one of these
wonders of frivolity.[30]

Despite the constant increase in productivity, the glove market
was still far from saturated, and the same 1878 exhibition report
commented that only if they used sewing machines would glove-
makers be able to keep up with an ever-growing demand. The
majority of French gloves sold that year were indeed machine
stitched.[31]

As gloves became increasingly ubiquitous, they generated
their own accessories, some simple, others ornate. They included
not only glove-stretchers, but button hooks, talcum-powder
shakers and decorative, lockable glove boxes that emphasized
the value placed on what had become an iconic article of dress.
Some fortunate little girls even had their own tiny versions of
these accessories to go with their dolls' miniature leather gloves.

Images of glove manufacture began to make their way into
nineteenth-century literature as writers came to recognize the
process's imaginative potential. Ellen Wood, the author of

immensely popular Victorian novels, whose father owned a large gloving business in Worcester, drew on her intimate knowledge of the industry to create a vivid social context for several of her books. In *Mrs Halliburton's Troubles* she goes to great lengths to describe the complexity of the glove-making process in the town of Hestonleigh (a thinly disguised Worcester), starting with the preparation of the leather:

Glove box made of sandalwood veneered with ivory and with a silvered brass lock, from around 1855. Elaborate glove boxes are an indication of the value placed on fine gloves.

> When the skins came in from the leather-dressers they were washed in a tub of cold water. The next day warm water, mixed with yolks of eggs, was poured on them, and a couple of men, bare-legged to the knee, got into the tub, and danced upon them, skins, eggs and water, for two hours. Then they were spread in a field to dry, till they were as hard as lantern horn; then they were 'staked', as it was called – a long process, to smooth and soften them. To the stainers next, to be stained black or coloured; next to the parers, to have the loose flesh pared from the inside, and to be smoothed again with pumice-stone – all this being done on the outside premises. Then they came inside, to the hands of one of the foremen, who sorted and marked them for the cutters. The cutters cut the skins into tranks (the shape of the hand in outline) with the separate thumbs and forgits, and sent them

in to the slitters. The slitters slit the four fingers, and *shaped* the thumbs and forgits: after that, they were ready for the women – three different women . . . being necessary to turn out each glove, so far as the sewing went; for one woman rarely worked at more than her own peculiar branch, or was capable of working at it. This done, and back in the manufactory again, they had to be pulled straight, and 'padded', or rubbed, a process by which they were brightened. If black gloves, the seams were washed over with a black dye, or else glazed; then they were hung up to dry.

Accessories for a doll, including tiny 12-button gloves and miniature glove stretchers, 19th century.

> This done, they . . . were sorted into firsts, seconds
> or thirds . . . It was called 'making-up'. Next they
> were banded round with a paper in dozens, labelled,
> and placed in small boxes, ready for the warehouses
> in London. A great deal, you see, before one pair of
> gloves could be turned out.[32]

Urine, or hens' or pigeons' droppings, or dogs' excrement were all involved in the process of making the skins more supple and receptive to dye, but Wood does not mention these less wholesome stages in the preparation of glove leather. Instead it is the work of the women that particularly interests her, as she drives home her message that glove-making brings important social benefits to the town's 'gloveresses'.

Glove-making had always been a gendered occupation. Men did the leather-cutting, because stretching the skins to ensure that gloves would keep their shape demanded much physical strength, whereas women did the stitching and embroidery, usually in their homes. Like the artist George William Mote (1832–1909), whose painting *Glovemaking* conveys calm contentment in its depiction of a woman with a gloving donkey sitting outside her cottage and sewing a glove in dappled sunshine, Wood paints an idyllic, summery picture of

> the women at their open doors and windows, busy
> over their nice clean work. Rocking the cradle with
> one foot, or jogging the baby on their knees, to a
> tune of their own composing, their hands would
> be ever active at their employment. Some made the
> gloves; that is, seamed the fingers together and put
> in the thumbs, and these were called 'makers'. Some
> welted, or hemmed the gloves round at the edge of
> the wrist; these were called 'welters'. Some worked
> the three ornamental lines on the back; and these

were called 'pointers'. Some of the work was done
in what was called a patent machine, whereby the
stitches were rendered perfectly equal. And some
of the stouter gloves were stitched together, instead
of being sewn: stitching so beautifully regular and
neat, that a stranger would look at it in admiration.
In short, there were, and are, different branches
in the making and sewing of gloves, as there are
in most trades.[33]

Wood is eager for her readers to appreciate their own gloves and
to understand how much work went into their creation. But in
another example of the ways in which gloves take on new meaning, she is also determined to imbue their making with moral
value, and to represent the industry as a force for social good.
Cleanliness, order, dedication, cooperation and modesty are all
implicit in her descriptions of female workers such as Charlotte,
who sew the gloves that Wood's readers may have taken for
granted:

Charlotte was a glove-maker; that is, she sewed the
fingers together, and put in the thumbs, forgits and
quirks. Look at your own gloves, English made.
The long strips running up inside the fingers, are
the forgits; and the little pieces between, where the
fingers open, are the quirks. The gloves Charlotte was
occupied with now, were of a very dark green colour,
almost black, called corbeau in the trade, and they
were sewn with white silk. Charlotte's stitches were
as beautifully regular as though she had used a patent
machine. The white silk and the fellow glove to the one
she was making, lay inside a clean white handkerchief
doubled upon her lap; other gloves, equally well
covered, were in a basket at her side.[34]

Glovemaking by George William Mote (1832–1909), oil on canvas.
A gloving donkey stands next to a rural glove-stitcher, whose cottage has
long, low windows to provide light at the right height for indoor glove work.

Although Wood acknowledges that a few of these 'gloveresses' were slatterns who 'gave their husbands the welcome of a home of discomfort, ill-management and dirt', and that some of the male workers squandered their wages on drink, she depicts glove-making as socially and spiritually beneficial:

> It is a trade that may be said to be a blessing to the localities where it is carried on, since it is one of the very few employments that furnish to the poor female population easy, clean and profitable work *at their own homes*.[35]

Three paper strips for wrapping packets of French gloves. Top: gloves spill from two cornucopias. Middle: two women watch as a third stitches gloves outdoors; and a glove shop interior. Bottom: men preparing the glove leather. Glove-making was a gendered occupation.

Glove-making is represented as a public asset, an honest and respectable means for both sexes to earn a decent living without neglecting their children. In the novel, diligent glove-making saves the widowed Mrs Halliburton from destitution, and by the end her equally conscientious and upright son stands to inherit the town's large glove factory. With him at the helm, Wood implies, the Christian values embodied by the industry will be perpetuated.

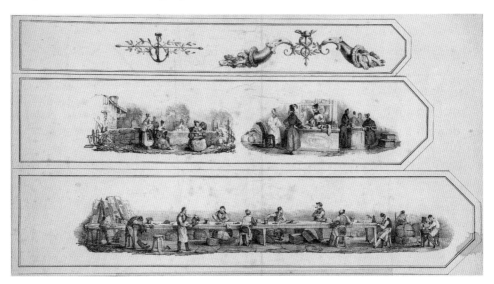

Glove-making provides a similarly ethical context for Walter Scott's 1828 novel *The Fair Maid of Perth,* which is set in late fourteenth-century Scotland, in a town whose glovers had formed themselves into an organized body several centuries earlier. Unlike Ellen Wood, Scott does not go into detail about how gloves are made; nor is their manufacture central to the plot. But the main character, Simon Glover, who 'derived his name from the trade which he practised', is presented as the embodiment of honesty and integrity, attributes inextricably linked to his glove-making.[36] Repeatedly referred to as 'the honest glover' or 'the good glover', Glover asserts that 'a glove is the emblem of faith, and a man of my craft should therefore less than any other break his own.'[37] Scott depicts glove-making as a profoundly honourable occupation, for, as Glover argues, unlike a shoe, a glove possesses all the virtuous qualities associated with the hand:

> Bethink you, that we employ the hands as pledges of friendship and good faith, and the feet have no such privilege. Brave men fight with their hands – cowards employ their feet in flight. A glove is borne aloft, a shoe is trampled in the mire – a man greets a friend with his open hand; he spurns a dog, or one whom he holds as mean as a dog, with his advanced foot. A glove on the point of a spear is a sign and pledge of faith all the wide world over, as a gauntlet flung down is a gage of knightly battle.[38]

Throughout this novel gloves and glove-making are depicted as touchstones for probity. Glover swears 'by my honest word, and by the best glove I ever made', or 'by needle and buckskin'; his own honour is never in doubt.[39] Moreover he uses a pair of his expertly crafted gloves to unite his daughter Catherine (the 'fair maid') with her shy suitor, Henry Gow. Reminding Gow

of the old custom whereby 'the maiden who ventures to kiss a
sleeping man wins of him a pair of gloves,' Glover provides him
with 'a pair of delicate kid-skin, that will exactly suit her hand
and arm'.[40] In a trope reminiscent of the slipper that will fit no
one but Cinderella, Glover assures Gow that, 'except Catherine,
I know not the woman in Scotland whom they would fit, though
I have measured most of the high beauties of the court.'[41] As
Gow encourages Catherine to put on the gloves, he implies that
their perfect craftsmanship and fit are proof that she has full
paternal approval for their love match:

> Look at that taper arm . . . look at these small fingers;
> think who sewed these seams of silk and gold, and
> think whether the glove, and the arm which alone
> the glove can fit ought to remain separate.[42]

French nineteenth-century novelists also weave depictions
of glove-making into their fiction in order to convey moral
values, but in contrast to their British counterparts, they tend
to show the industry in an unfavourable light. In *Germinie
Lacerteux* (1865) the Goncourt brothers portray the thoroughly
unpleasant Jupillon as an indolent and pretentious glove-cutter
who puts on airs whenever a passer-by pauses to watch him
at work in the window of a Parisian glove shop. In Gérard de
Nerval's *Sylvie* (1853), the fact that the central character aban-
dons her delicate lacemaking to become a glove-maker who
turns out gloves using a *mécanique* is seen as emblematic of the
country's declining values and lost innocence. And in stark contrast to *Mrs Halliburton's Troubles*, Elie Berthet's *Le Gouffre*
(The Abyss; 1872) depicts the negative side of glove-making.
While acknowledging that stitching gloves may bring certain
benefits to women living in the countryside around Grenoble,
Berthet shows how the arrival of this new industry overwhelms
the local inhabitants and their traditional way of life.[43] He

contrasts the situation of girls who work in Grenoble itself, sewing by machine and producing a dozen gloves a day, with the pitiful income and wretched working conditions of a poor, sick, rural glove-stitcher who has to sew by hand for fourteen hours in order to earn a pitiful 20 sous.[44]

As these novels show, the glove industry affected social organization in many different ways. Intersecting with ethics, politics, gender and class, it provided skilled employment for women as well as men, and contributed to the regeneration – or in some cases the decline – of regional prosperity. It boosted demand for skins and for the supplies and skills needed to turn them into fine glove leather. It even influenced architecture. Long, low windows were cut into cottage walls at the right height to provide more daylight for the rural glove-worker (as can be seen in Mote's painting *Glovemaking*); in towns such as Grenoble, rows of tall houses were built with glove workshops on the top floors for the best light, while the family lived downstairs; and later, purpose-built factories were designed with many tall windows for maximum illumination.

But the industry also had a darker social impact, for in the closing decades of the nineteenth century it began to be recognized that glove-making could take a dreadful toll on workers' health. Anthrax, often fatal, was a constant risk when handling the skins. Some types of liquid dyes were brushed directly on to gloves in a solution that was equally toxic to worker and wearer. An English account from 1871 tells of a woman who suffered from repeated skin ulcerations around her fingernails after purchasing 'a box of green-coloured gloves at a well-known and respectable house'; the gloves were found to be impregnated with arsenic salts.[45] Even the process of cleaning gloves was hazardous. Applying in 1917 for a patent for a machine to dry and deodorize gloves after they had been cleaned, its inventor explained that

Nov. 24, 1925·

R. GOLTMAN

1,562,631

GLOVE STRETCHER, POWDERER, AND HEATER

Filed Jan. 22, 1925

3 Sheets-Sheet 1

Inventor
Rebecca Goltman

By William Clinton
Attorney

A 1925 patent for a device to stretch, powder and heat gloves.

Prior to this invention kid gloves have generally been
cleaned in benzin and after having been taken from
the benzin, attendants, usually girls, blow into the
gloves for the purpose of distending them into a
smooth form, and then the gloves are hung up to
dry. This method is very tedious and slow, often
causing the skin about the mouth to become sore
and disfigured.[46]

Previous types of drying machine, he added, had been liable
to explode.

Clearly, the glove industry was not always the benevolent
force that Ellen Wood implied. Her sanguine account could
hardly be more different from the image of glove-making that
emerges from a French medical treatise of 1883, whose author not
only details the permanent deformities that the industry's chemicals and processes could inflict on workers' hands, but shows
that leather glove-workers had one of the lowest life expectancies
of all artisans. Their average age at death was only 31, and more
than 70 per cent of those deaths were from pneumonia, caused
by working in an environment full of leather dust.[47]

In the twenty-first century most glove production has
changed beyond recognition. Few gloves are still created entirely
by hand using traditional methods, although some small family-
run businesses, particularly in Italy, continue to make leather
gloves as they have done for generations. For several companies,
the expert hand-craftsmanship of their high-quality gloves is
the main selling point. One such example is Sermoneta in Italy,
which advertises 'haute couture for the hands', and emphasizes
traditional skills and workmanship:

To produce a pair of Sermoneta gloves, 28 processing
steps are required, combined with the skill and
precision of at least ten craftsmen who, with expert

hands, create patterns, cut and pack the leather . . .
Only Sermoneta's craftsmanship can guarantee the
anatomical perfection of the lines that perfectly follow
the contours of the hand.[48]

So, too, does Dents in England, a company established in 1777
and proud to advertise that in its eco-friendly Warminster
factory,

> craftsmen follow the time-honoured traditions needed
> to produce the world's best gloves. Involving as many
> as 32 stages and taking up to eight hours to make,
> each hand cut, handstitched pair of gloves gets the
> same VIP treatment.[49]

Renewed interest in the allure of luxurious, high-fashion
gloves keeps specialist manufacturers in business. However, in
many former gloving centres, such as Gloversville in upstate
New York, which once called itself the 'glove-making capital of
the world' and turned out nearly 90 per cent of the gloves made
in the United States, few gloves, if any, are now produced. The
same is true of Worcester, once at the heart of British glove-
making. Leather gloves for Pittards of Yeovil are now made in
their factories in Ethiopia. Traditional glove-making is on the
British Heritage Crafts Association's Red List of endangered
crafts, and the association estimates that in the UK fewer than
one hundred individuals still derive their main income from
making gloves.

Today, most glove mass production has moved away from
Europe and America, mainly to Asia, and output is dominated
by disposable medical gloves. Thin rubber gloves for medical
purposes were first introduced in the 1880s, initially to protect
the hands of operating theatre staff from harsh disinfectants.
They were then produced in sterile form for use in surgery, but

the mass production of disposable latex gloves began in the 1960s. Now they are manufactured in unimaginably large numbers and in a variety of other materials including nitrile, vinyl and thermoplastic elastomer. Nothing could be further from traditional glove-making techniques than the long rows of ceramic or aluminium hand-shaped moulds that glide through huge factories on conveyor belts, gracefully turning this way and that as they dip into a series of chemical solutions before being baked, washed, dried and brushed until a glove is peeled off each one. In July 2019 the Top Glove Corporation of Malaysia, which advertises itself as 'The World's Largest Manufacturer of Gloves', reported that its factories had a combined glove production capacity of 62.7 billion pieces per annum.[50] That year, global demand for medical gloves reached 290 billion, a figure far outstripped since then as governments around the world clamoured for supplies to help combat the COVID-19 pandemic.

Such changes have an inevitable impact on those working in glove manufacture. One of the most insightful explorations of

Rows of hand-shaped moulds move through a series of factory processes to create disposable medical gloves. Hundreds of billions of disposable gloves are produced each year.

the changing glove industry's wider cultural ramifications comes in Philip Roth's 1997 novel *American Pastoral*. The glove industry is central to the book, which charts the changing American psyche by following several generations of the Levov family's glove business, from the late nineteenth century through the complacent optimism of the 1950s to the chaos and confusion of the Vietnam War years.

The changing fortunes of country and family are mapped against changes in glove fashions and production methods. The first Mr Levov arrives in New Jersey in the 1890s and finds work fleshing sheepskin in a tannery; his son ships hides to be tanned in Gloversville, by then the centre of the American glove trade, and he starts to employ families of new Italian immigrants to cut and stitch kid gloves in a small Newark loft. Roth's description of the traditional methods used by the original immigrant workers conveys a sense of multi-generational domestic harmony that will later be lacking not only in the Levov family but in the nation as a whole:

> The old Italian grandfather or the father did the
> cutting on the kitchen table, with the French rule,
> the shears, and the spud knife he'd brought from Italy.
> The grandmother or the mother did the sewing, and
> the daughters did the laying off – ironing the glove –
> in the old-fashioned way, with irons heated up in a box
> set atop the kitchen's potbellied stove.[51]

It remains a marginal business until 1942, when the u.s. Army places a huge order for black, lined, sheepskin dress gloves. Lou Levov 'knew how to cut a glove, knew how to cut a deal' and by the end of the war he has been so successful at both that he opens a second factory in Puerto Rico.[52] There the tranquil domesticity of the handmade glove process gives way to the dehumanized din of post-war industrial mass production:

'You can't imagine the noise out there, the sewing machines whining, the clicking machines pounding, hundreds of machines going all at once.'[53]

Lou Levov sits at his desk at the centre of the factory floor, a dominant power surveying the workers and controlling his domain.[54] His glove factories embody the optimism of America's booming economy and political supremacy, and his faith in the great American Dream is expressed in terms of glove-making. Later, however, he will look back wistfully to the 'old-style world', when

it was nothing for an ordinary woman to own twenty, twenty-five pair of gloves. Quite common. A woman used to have a glove wardrobe, different gloves for every outfit – different colours, different styles, different lengths. A woman wouldn't go outside without a pair in any weather. In those days it wasn't unusual for a woman to spend two, three hours at the glove counter and try on thirty pair of gloves, and the lady behind the desk had a sink and she would wash her hands between each color.[55]

With almost religious fervour, Levov pursues a quest for perfection, both in his family and in his business, through rigorous quality control. When his son is between the ages of six and nine, he subjects him to a glove catechism every Saturday morning, in an attempt to ensure that the next generation will be inculcated with the same values and convictions as his own:

'What is calfskin, Seymour?' 'The skin from young calves.' 'What kind of grain?' 'It has a tight, even grain. Very smooth. Glossy.' 'What's it used for?' 'Mostly for men's gloves. It's heavy.' 'What is Cape?' 'The skin of the South African haired sheep.' 'Cabretta?' 'Not the

Female factory workers sewing gloves by machine in Gloversville, New York, in 1938. Calling itself 'the glove-making capital of the world', Gloversville produced nearly 90 per cent of the gloves sold in the u.s. between 1890 and 1950.

wool-type sheep but the hair-type sheep.' 'From where?' 'South America. Brazil.' 'That's part of the answer. The animals live a little north and south of the equator. Anywhere around the world. Southern India. Northern Brazil. A band across Africa –' 'We got ours from *Brazil*.' 'Right. That's true. You're right. I'm only telling you they come from other countries too. So you'll know. What's the key operation in preparing the skin?' 'Stretching.' 'And never forget it. In this business, a sixteenth of an inch makes all the difference in the world. Stretching! Stretching is a hundred per cent right. How many parts in a pair of gloves?' 'Ten, twelve if there's a binding.' 'Name 'em.' 'Six fourchettes, two thumbs, two tranks.' 'The unit of measurement in the glove trade?' 'Buttons.' 'What's a one-button glove?' 'A one-button glove in one inch long if you measure from the base of the thumb to the top.' 'Approximately one inch long. What is silking?' 'The

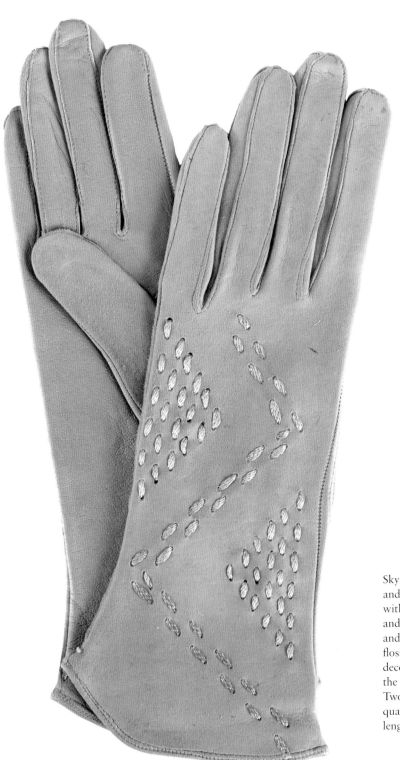

Sky-blue suede and kid gloves with quirks and fourchettes and with blue floss silk thread decoration on the back, 1920s. Two-and-three-quarter button length.

three rows of stitching on the back of the glove. If you don't do the end pulling, all the silking is going to come right out.' 'Excellent. I didn't even ask you about end pulling. Excellent. What's the most difficult seam to make on a glove?' 'Full piqué.' 'Why? Take your time, son – it's difficult. Tell me why.' The prixseam. The gauge seam. Single draw points. Spear points. Buckskin. Mocha. English does. Soaking. Dehairing. Pickling. Sorting. Taxing. The grain finish. The velvet finish. Pasted linings. Skeleton linings. Seamless knitted wool. Cut-and-sewed knitted wool.[56]

By the 1960s, however, gloves have fallen from fashion. Unable to compete with cheap labour in the Far East, American glove manufacturing went into a decline that for Roth symbolizes the wider erosion of American power and influence: 'Even baseball gloves, the most American glove of all . . . for a long time now had been manufactured in Korea.'[57]

Glove-making and politics continue to intertwine as Lou Levov associates the Kennedy presidency with a brief period of renewed hope for both the industry and the nation:

Thank God in 1960 Jackie Kennedy walked out there with a little glove to the wrist, and a glove to the elbow, and a pillbox hat, and all of a sudden gloves were in style again. First Lady of the glove industry . . . That woman put the ladies' fine leather glove back on the map. But when they assassinated Kennedy and Jacqueline Kennedy left the White House, that and the miniskirt was the end of the ladies' fashion glove. The assassination of John F. Kennedy and the arrival of the miniskirt, and together that was the death knell for the ladies' dress glove. Till then it was a twelve-month, year-round business.[58]

Optimism and certainty turn sour as the American glove trade collapses, mirroring Kennedy's assassination, the disintegration of the Levov family and a nation beset by conflict and decline:

> Manufacturing is finished in Newark . . . And gloves?
> In America? Kaput. Also finished . . . Five more years
> and outside of the government contracts there won't
> be a pair of gloves made in America. Not in Puerto
> Rico either. They're already in the Philippines, the
> big boys. It will be India, it'll be Indonesia, Pakistan,
> Bangladesh – you'll see, every place around the world
> making gloves except here.[59]

By the end of the novel, Levov recognizes his helplessness as his world falls apart. Roth shows him forced to accept that his ability to control every detail of a glove's construction, on which he had once so prided himself, is insufficient to hold back the series of failures he sees around him:

> He could not prevent anything. He never could,
> though only now did he look prepared to believe that
> manufacturing a superb ladies' dress glove in quarter
> sizes did not guarantee the making of a life that would
> fit to perfection everyone he loved. Far from it . . . The
> old system that made order doesn't work anymore.[60]

Although Levov can no longer explain the world to himself through the reassuring prism of glove-making, for his creator, as for writers as diverse as Ellen Wood, Walter Scott and Elie Berthet, gloves and the details of their manufacture provided an imaginative means of tracing social change and exploring concepts of morality, integrity and idealism. Under their pens, accounts of the glove-making process did more than explain how gloves were made.

THREE

'Tear at the Thumb, Troubles to Come': The Language of Gloves

'The hands may almost be said to speak,' wrote the Roman rhetorician Quintilian towards the end of the first century AD; 'they are almost as expressive as words.'[1] But if a bare hand – gesticulating, stroking, waving, pointing – is adept at conveying meaning, a gloved hand can be an even more effective means of communication, even when still. Small but highly visible, adaptable to different materials and embellishments, able to be put on and taken off in public unlike other items of clothing, gloves are ideally suited to projecting information. A finely embroidered, perfumed and beribboned glove announces different things about its owner than a dirty, scuffed one with split seams. But gloves can do more than articulate distinctions in wealth or status, for they adapt to the wearer's hands, absorb their physical traces and reveal something of the owner's temperament. As the French art historian Charles Blanc observed in 1875, 'What a lot there is in an item that has been worn by a man's hand and still retains the imprint of his nervous movements and trembling fingers while he was lost in thought.'[2] Blanc was particularly alert to the expressivity of a gloved hand, and expressed concern that gloves of the wrong colour would impair the hand's articulacy: 'Unless they are a sign of mourning, black gloves are unacceptable because, as if under a layer of ink, they obliterate the hand, that most perfect instrument of universal language.'[3]

The communicative potential of gloves has been exploited in ingenious ways that encourage the hand to 'speak' more clearly than Quintilian could ever have imagined. A particularly striking example comes in the form of an English broadside from the 1560s, which depicts a pair of gloves overprinted with powerful Christian lessons. The text describes them as:

> Some fine gloves devised for New Year's gifts to teach young people to know good from evil, whereby they may learn the Ten Commandments at their fingers' ends. Ten other good lessons be written within the fingers, the tree of virtues with her branches in the right palm and the root of vices in the left.

The gloves have been torn 'by impatient breath' and can be repaired only by the 'fear and love' of God, represented by an accompanying needle and thread. The broadside claims, however, that long contemplation of the text inscribed on their fingers and palms will cause for the recipient of the gloves 'all evil in time to lay full low'.[4]

Other examples offer practical rather than spiritual instruction. In 1680 the Scottish linguist George Dalgarno published his *Didascalocophus; or, The Deaf and Dumb Man's Tutor*, in which he proposed a new linguistic system for use by deaf mutes. His method involved allocating the letters of the alphabet to specific points on the hand, which could be touched to spell out words. To make things easier for young beginners, he instructed that

> a pair of Gloves be made, one for the Master and another for the Scholar, with the letters written upon them in such order as appears in the following Scheme. To practice with these, will be easy for any that do but know their letters and can spell; and a short time will so fix the places of the letters in the Memory, that the Gloves may be thrown away as useless.[5]

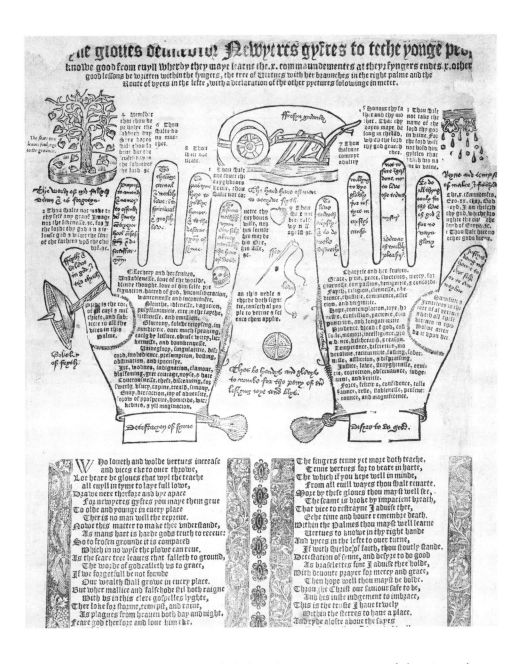

This London broadside from the 1560s uses an image of gloves 'to teach young people to know good from evil'. The torn glove can be repaired only by the 'fear and love' of God, represented by needle and thread.

Various versions of Dalgarno's glove have been created since, including one developed at the end of the nineteenth century by the inventor Alexander Graham Bell, who devised a modified example to help the young deaf and blind Helen Keller to communicate; she is known to have asked for 'some beautiful gloves to talk with'.[6]

The idea that gloves can 'talk' is central to an anonymous modern retelling of the Cinderella story, recorded by Carol Padden and Tom Humphries in *Deaf in America* (1990). In this version, a profoundly deaf Cinderella is given a pair of glass gloves by her fairy godmother. These enable her to sign so elegantly and effortlessly that she captures the heart of her 'prince', and a glass glove lost at midnight leads to the tale's traditional happy ending and a bride who can now communicate fluently.[7]

The ability of the garments to communicate continues to be explored in less fanciful ways. Twenty-first-century versions of the talking glove are being developed, including some with motion sensors that detect the shapes and movements made by the wearer's hand when he or she uses American Sign Language (ASL). The gloves convert ASL's 26 letters into text on

'Talking Glove' devised by the deaf-blind American author Morrison Heady (1829–1915). It enabled people to communicate with the wearer by touching the letters printed on it.

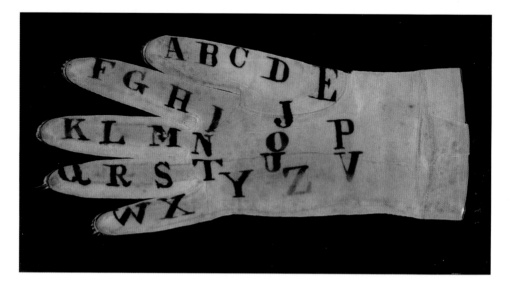

a smartphone, allowing profoundly deaf users to communicate with people unfamiliar with signing.[8]

The anonymous Frenchman mentioned in Chapter Two who altered the wording on his gloves from 'Vive le roi' to 'Vive la loi' was all too aware that his gloves were legible. 'Long live the law' was not the only message to be read on chamois leather gloves in the early years of the French Revolution, however, when it was not uncommon for gloves to proclaim their wearer's political affiliations with printed slogans such as 'Vive la nation, l'union, la liberté, 1789' (Long live nation, union and liberty, 1789), or with a pointed vignette of 'Liberty Sitting at the Altar of Peace'.[9] When the Marquis de Lafayette toured America in 1824–5, gloves stamped with his portrait advertised the wearer's support for the hero of the American Revolution. And after the death of the Bourbon king Charles x in 1836, certain Parisian opportunists are said to have used their gloves to signal their political allegiance, taking both black and yellow pairs to the theatre or opera so that they could extend a hand in mourning if they met a Legitimist, but appear conventionally gloved for Orleanist acquaintances.[10]

Political messages have continued to be expressed by gloves, sometimes very directly, as in the case of gloves produced for Dwight Eisenhower's American presidential campaign in 1952, which were printed with a repeating pattern that read 'I like IKE'. But indirect messaging could be just as effective. During the medal ceremony at the 1968 Olympic Games, African American athletes Tommie Smith and John Carlos famously gave a clenched-fist salute on the podium. Both men had intended to bring black gloves for their protest, but Carlos forgot his and had to borrow Smith's left glove and raise his left hand. Smith later said that he had raised his right gloved fist to represent Black Power in America, while Carlos had raised his left to represent Black unity, so that together the two black-gloved fists formed an arch of unity and power.[11]

Woman's glove printed with a portrait of the Marquis de Lafayette. Several similar versions were produced to commemorate Lafayette's grand tour of the U.S. in 1824–5.

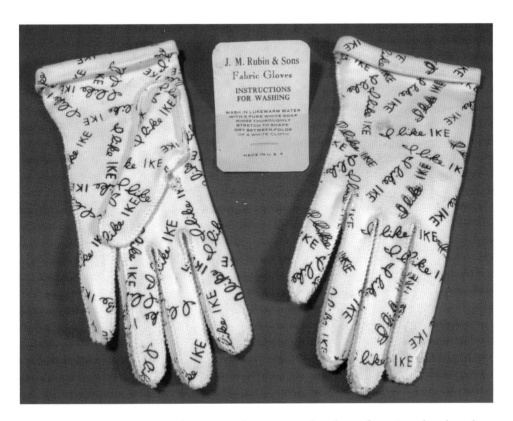

Women's gloves printed with 'I like IKE' in blue and red, made for supporters of Dwight D. Eisenhower's 1952 American presidential campaign.

At other times the message has been functional rather than political, like that carried by gloves produced in 1851 for visitors to London's Great Exhibition. Printed with a diagrammatic map, they were designed to help wearers navigate between the city's main landmarks and the Crystal Palace exhibition site by consulting their hands.

More recently, in the world of high fashion John Galliano's 2001 leather newspaper-print gloves embraced the idea that gloves can literally be read. Imprinted with 'news' from the '*Galliano Gazette*', they came packed in elegantly matching newsprint tissue and glove box. Major designers often add identifying signatures to their luxury gloves, aware that the wearer will want them to be read and recognized as status symbols. Chanel produces gloves embossed with a large CC logo; Louis

Athletes Tommie
Smith and John
Carlos raise
fists clad in
black gloves to
demonstrate
support for Black
Power during their
medal ceremony
at the Mexico
City Olympics in
1968.

Vuitton's are printed with the familiar LV initials; Valentino's
come decorated with a characteristic V; Dior's spell out the
brand name and add a dangling gilt D for good measure; and
Versace sells black leather gloves embroidered with Gianni
Versace's signature in white. For a wider market, the messages
recently spelled out by knitted gloves from the British department store John Lewis were equally legible: their paired palms
read either 'HEY' and 'YOU', or 'BE' and 'MINE'.

Usually, however, the language of gloves is less literal. They
are adept at sending out silent visual messages, though sometimes at the risk of misinterpretation. After the city of Florence
passed a law in 1388 decreeing that all prostitutes had to wear
gloves in public, it is said that respectable Florentine women
became reluctant to wear any for fear of being mistaken for
whores.[12] But prostitutes' gloves continued to sow confusion.
By the sixteenth century, their expensively gloved hands were
sending out such socially misleading signals that the government of Bologna banned them from wearing 'embroidered or
perfumed gloves' in an attempt to distinguish them from the
town's elite.[13]

Newsprint-patterned kid gloves by John Galliano with matching box and tissue, 2001.

Concern that gloves should not convey disreputable signals led Jean-Baptiste de la Salle, a French priest and founder of the country's first Catholic schools, to include strict advice on glove-wearing in his *Règles de la bienséance et de la civilité chrétiennes* (Rules of Christian Propriety and Civility), a 1695 treatise aimed at schoolchildren. He was determined that their glove-wearing habits should be consistent with the highest social and moral standards of behaviour:

> It is good manners to have gloves on your hands when you are out in the street, when you are in company, and when you go to the country; it is improper to hold them in your hand, wave them about, play with them, or use them to hit someone; that is schoolboy behaviour.
>
> Gloves must be removed on entering a church, before taking holy water, before praying to God, and before sitting down at table. When you wish to greet someone by making a deep bow or kissing their hand, you should be bare-handed, and removing the right-hand glove is enough; that is also what good manners require before something is given or received.
>
> In company it is bad manners to keep pulling gloves on and off; it is also impolite to lift them to your mouth to bite or suck them, or to carry them under the left arm, or to wear only the left glove and to hold the other glove in that hand, or to put them in your pocket when they ought to be on your hands.[14]

De la Salle asserts that his advice is based on Christian principles: modesty and respect for others were paramount, and proper glove use was a sign of adherence to those principles. His rules put great emphasis on when gloves should be worn and when they should be removed. While he stipulates that hands should always be covered in public, he makes clear that the removal of one or both gloves is a sign of deference, either to a person or to God. Pulling gloves on and off at random was unacceptable behaviour because it undermined that moral code.

Although de la Salle's glove-wearing strictures may appear comprehensive, they were to be surpassed by the prescriptions about glove-wearing that developed in the nineteenth century, particularly in France. Diderot and d'Alembert's *Encyclopédie* of 1751 had defined a glove simply as a type of winter garment intended to protect hands from the cold, but ever-increasing layers of meaning overwhelmed that basic function in the century that followed.

Georges Guenot-Lecointe analysed the phenomenon at length in his *Physiologie du gant* (Physiology of the Glove), published in 1841, where he claimed that the remarkable changes he had seen in glove-manufacturing even by that date were emblematic of a change in France itself: they indicated an evolution from barbarism to civilization. For him, the old days of badly stitched gloves before the introduction of the *mécanique* evoked the 'first centuries of barbarism', whereas a well-made straw-coloured glove was 'the most advanced expression of modern civilization'.[15] Conscious that a fundamental change was taking place around him, Guenot-Lecointe comments that in the early years of the nineteenth century gloves had relatively limited social significance – he says they 'played only a very minor role in our habits; they were rarely mentioned, and . . . no-one paid much attention to them'.[16] By the time he published his *Physiologie*, however, the glove had 'invaded all social classes'.[17]

The increasingly nuanced messages conveyed by gloves in the nineteenth century may be attributed to that 'invasion'. With new manufacturing techniques making gloves more readily available to wider sections of society, by the 1840s glove-wearing was no longer the preserve of the elite. More than ever, gloves

acted as subtle social markers, sending out discreet messages to those sufficiently well bred to decipher them. 'The glove alone indicates which rung we occupy on Jacob's ladder,' wrote Guenot-Lecointe, and with a growing and aspirational middle class increasingly eager to adopt them as a mark of their new status, gloves became a tool to help their wearers position themselves favourably within a rapidly changing social hierarchy.[18] To the lower classes, gloves were an enviable emblem of leisured affluence. 'To working-class children, gloves mean dignity; they represent luxury *par excellence*, they are a symptom of leisure!', commented the socially influential French writer Delphine de Girardin in 1837, observing that little girls were delighted to be given cast-off gloves to play with because for them, 'old gloves are something to be proud of.'[19] To the middle classes, glove-wearing had come to seem indispensable – in 1846 Gustave Flaubert noted that people would rather go out without money than without gloves.[20] And according to the journalist Eugène

George Clausen, *Schoolgirls, Haverstock Hill*, 1880, oil on canvas. Difference in social status is underlined by the contrast between the gloved hands of the middle-class girls and the bare hands of the street sellers.

Chapus, writing under the aristocratic-sounding pseudonym of Vicomte de Marennes, the gloves of a well-dressed man could instantly tell an onlooker what he was about to do.[21]

Although some commentators claimed that the increasing ubiquity of gloves represented a new, classless egalitarianism, most recognized that, on the contrary, subtle variations in how they were worn revealed crucial social differences. Deciphering the language of gloves was a skill not shared by all, however. Delphine de Girardin mocked those who were ignorant of such subtleties and whose gloves betrayed their undistinguished social origins, tartly observing that some men seemed to think that they could win an heiress's hand in marriage simply by putting on white gloves and a black coat.[22] The mere fact of wearing gloves was not enough to claim social distinction: it was knowing which ones to wear, and when and how to wear them, that showed where one stood in the social hierarchy. It is not surprising, then, that as glove production and ownership grew, so did the number of publications offering advice on an increasingly elaborate set of prescriptions and prohibitions surrounding glove-wearing.

Deciding which gloves to buy was the first hurdle. 'Very few persons are careful enough in selecting gloves,' announced Samuel R. Wells, the American author of *How to Behave*, in the condescending tones characteristic of many etiquette manuals.[23] Choice of colour and material were crucial. 'Never let your gloves be of any material that is not kid or calf. Worsted or cotton gloves are unutterably vulgar,' declared the British publisher George Routledge in *Routledge's Manual of Etiquette*.[24]

For Guenot-Lecointe, the colour of gloves was 'an almost infallible indication of their owner's intimate habits'.[25] He noted that kid gloves came in an infinite variety of shades, each projecting its own meaning: a dandy's gloves could tell you where he was about to go and what he was about to do without a word being spoken. Certain basic rules pertained when selecting the colour. Darker gloves were worn during the day, and paler ones in the evening, when to be seen in dark gloves was considered 'an abomination'.[26] Women, however, were advised to avoid very pale gloves on the grounds that they might distract from the beauty of their pale complexions.[27] In a culture that set great store by the whiteness of a woman's skin, the French writer Madame Celnart warned dark-skinned women that the contrast with white gloves was 'really intolerable', and in terms that are shocking to a modern reader, suggested they instead wear long flesh-coloured gloves of thick crêpe to hide what she called 'that horrid shade'.[28] A British etiquette manual, published in 1859, reminded readers that 'our great-grandmothers . . . had their white kid gloves sewn to the bottom of each sleeve, lest they should incur the calamity of a sun-burnt arm.'[29] It was doubtless to avoid such a 'calamity' that Lydia Cassatt,

Mary Cassatt, *Lydia Crocheting in the Garden at Marly*, 1880, oil on canvas. Even when using her fingers for delicate needlework, Lydia wears gloves outdoors as etiquette required.

in a portrait by her sister Mary, wears long gloves as she sits crocheting in a summer garden, although needlework cannot have been easy with gloved fingers.

Yellow gloves – particularly favoured by dandies and earning them their French nickname of *gants jaunes* – represented the peak of modern civilization to Guenot-Lecointe.[30] They remained fashionable throughout the nineteenth century: maize- or straw-coloured for the morning; paler cream for evening. Neutral colours such as pearl-grey or putty were also deemed acceptable for men and women, although Charles Blanc advised against tones such as steel-grey, bronze or slate because they were colours associated with unyielding materials, and so might detract from the glove's essential quality of suppleness.[31] On the other hand, brighter tones such as oxblood, violet, poppy or green – especially green – were a sign of vulgarity or petit-bourgeois provincialism when worn by either sex.[32] 'Bright-colored gloves bring the hands into too much conspicuousness for good effect, and . . . give the whole man a plebeian air,' Henry Lunettes told American readers.[33] Routledge gave full vent to his disapproval of ill-chosen shades in his *Manual of Etiquette*:

> Imagine a lady dressed in mauve silk, with a mauve bonnet, and *emerald green kid gloves*! or vice versa, in green silk, with a bonnet to match, and *mauve-coloured gloves*! Dark green, dark mauve, or plum coloured, dark salmon, or dark yellow gloves, are enough to spoil the most faultless costume; because they interrupt the harmony of colour; like the one string of a musical instrument, which, being out of tune, creates a discord throughout all the rest.[34]

A glove's fit was another indicator of distinction. 'Well-fitting gloves . . . tell of a neat and refined taste,' stated Routledge,

telling his readers that their 'gloves should fit to the last degree
of perfection'.[34] But if Madame Celnart had warned in 1833 that
it was 'unsightly and common to have gloves that are too wide',
later in the century a more frequent mistake was for women to
squeeze their hands into gloves that were too tight, in an attempt
to make them look daintier.[35] Pointing out that 'a container
is always greater than its contents,' commentators cautioned
their readers that forcing their hands into gloves that were too
small would have the opposite effect.[36] Gloves loudly proclaimed
class, unless the wearer was very careful. According to Baroness
Staffe, the author of dozens of French conduct manuals, as
gloves became more affordable, working-class men began to
wear them to disguise their calloused hands, but opted for gloves
so tight that they were in danger of stopping the circulation or
bursting apart.

Achieving an appropriate fit was not always easy, however, for not all shops offered the seductively attentive service
described by Émile Zola in *Au Bonheur des dames* (The Ladies'
Paradise; 1883):

In the glove department, a row of ladies were seated
at the narrow counter covered in green velvet and
edged with nickel. And before them, smiling
assistants piled up flat, bright pink boxes, which
they produced from under the counter as if from
the labelled drawers of a filing cabinet. Mignot
in particular was leaning forward with his pretty,
chubby face, and giving his thick Parisian accent
tender inflexions. He had already sold Mme
Desforges a dozen pairs of kid gloves – Bonheur
gloves, the speciality of the store. She had then
asked for three pairs of suede gloves. And now
she was trying on Saxe gloves, worrying they
might not be the right size.

'Oh! They fit you perfectly, madam!' repeated Mignot. 'The six-and-a-quarter would be too big for a hand like yours.'

Half-lying on the counter, he held her hand, taking her fingers one by one and sliding the glove on with a long, repeated, insistent caress. And he watched her as if expecting to see her face melt in voluptuous pleasure. But with her elbow on the edge of the velvet and her wrist raised, she surrendered her fingers to him as calmly as she yielded her foot to her chambermaid to have her boot buttons fastened.[37]

Although etiquette demanded the close fit that nineteenth-century developments in cut and new fastening devices had made possible, some glove merchants were unwilling to have fine gloves damaged by customers who tried them on without buying them. The 1864 edition of Eliza Leslie's *The Ladies' Guide to True Politeness and Perfect Manners* offered its American readers a practical solution:

It is not admissible to try on kid gloves in a store. After buying a pair, ask for the glove-stretcher (which they keep in all good shops, for the convenience of customers) and then stretch the gloves upon it, unless you have a glove-stretcher at home. This will render them easy to put on when you take them into wear. Glove-stretchers are to be bought at the variety stores; or ought to be. They will save many a new glove from tearing.[38]

Tight-fitting, fine leather gloves were prone to splitting, and it was unseemly to be seen in torn gloves. The need for care was reinforced by a superstitious rhyme that warned of a ripped glove's grim implications:

Tear at the thumb, troubles to come,
Tear at the finger, troubles linger,
Tear at the hand, troubles stand,
Don't tear at all, troubles won't fall.[39]

Being seen in torn gloves was to invite moral censure. One French advice manual warned that a girl whose gloves often split or tore was liable to turn into 'a disorderly woman'.[40] Even in the 1960s Australian schoolgirls, subjected to daily glove inspections by their teachers, tried to disguise holes in their navy gloves by inking over the exposed skin with fountain pens to avoid punishment.[41] In the nineteenth century, however, there was one circumstance in which burst seams were forgivable and even admirable. Gloves that split during enthusiastic applause at the theatre were felt to be an expression of the wearer's sensitive and passionate nature. If a performance has been outstanding, wrote Champfleury, 'applause is then a sacred duty; the proprieties need no longer be respected, one tears one's gloves and shouts, there has to be a violent eruption of emotion.'[42] No shame was attached to gloves ripped in such a context.

If a split seam was occasionally forgivable, wearing faded or soiled gloves was beyond the pale. Staining was a hazard of nineteenth-century theatre-going, and women were advised to 'avoid handling the playbills, as the printing ink will soil your gloves in a few minutes, making your hands appear very badly for the rest of the evening.'[43]

The French novelist Honoré de Balzac's comment that 'a tear is a misfortune, a stain is a vice' was particularly true of

Wooden Victorian glove stretchers for easing open the fingers of tight-fitting gloves. More luxurious versions were produced in silver or ivory.

A line of uniformed usherettes hold their white gloved hands up for inspection at the Roxy Theatre, New York, in 1945.

gloves, and commentators were quick to point out the class implications of such a transgression.[44] Routledge warned that 'a soiled pair of light gloves [is] to be scrupulously avoided by any young lady who is ambitious of preserving the exterior of a gentlewoman.'[45] And Baroness Staffe pronounced that there was no uglier sight than a soiled glove. The very idea was repugnant to her: she reminded her readers that well-bred ladies spoke of 'soiled gloves', never of 'dirty gloves', since the latter was a 'naturalist' term that evoked far too unpleasant an image.[46]

Although nineteenth-century manuals of good manners offered extensive advice on glove-cleaning, involving a variety of methods and substances ranging from toast crusts to cyanide, in the best circles wearing gloves that had been cleaned rather than discarded was unthinkable.[47] As Baroness Staffe noted, the only thing more repulsive than a torn glove was one that gave off the disgusting odour of benzene or ammonia cleaning fluid.[48]

Pierre-Auguste Renoir, *The Theatre Box*, 1874, oil on canvas. Wearing white or pale yellow gloves to the theatre was de rigueur for both sexes.

In fashionable society gloves therefore had the very briefest of lives. 'A cleaned glove is like a reheated dinner; it is never any good,' declared Guenot-Lecointe, explaining that the more often one changed one's gloves, the more highly one was regarded.[49] Doubtless this was why Flaubert once ended his light-hearted list of New Year's greetings to his teenage niece by wishing her 'fifteen billion pairs of new, butter-yellow gloves'.[50]

The pressure to conform to these strictures and ensure that one's covered hands sent out the right message is evident from repeated references in nineteenth-century French texts to 'des gants irréprochables' (irreproachable gloves). The freshness of one's gloves was perceived to be an indication of one's moral virtue, and so gloves, like their wearers, had to be beyond reproach. As Marennes put it, 'a glove sums up and expresses a host of moral inclinations.'[51] Yet it was beyond most people's means to discard gloves after only one wearing, like the ultra-fashionable elite whose elaborate glove-wearing rituals were summarized by the French writer and illustrator Bertall:

> The most elegant gentlemen change their gloves
> four or five times a day. Riding gloves in the morning,
> semi-formal gloves for going to lunch, formal kidskin
> or suede gloves for visits, dogskin gloves for driving
> in the Bois, gloves for dining in town, gloves for going
> to a ball, to the theatre or to a club in the evening.[52]

The equivalent Englishman was reputed to get through six pairs of gloves a day, which, if true, would have required enormous wealth.

Louise Colet's novel Ces Petits Messieurs (These Little Gentlemen; 1869) spells out the expense involved in trying to keep up appearances by maintaining a regular supply of fresh gloves over a long period, even on a less lavish scale:

the fashion was for straw-coloured gloves. A dandy
worthy of the name wore them even in broad daylight,
which meant two pairs of gloves every day: one pair
for afternoon visits, and another pair (at least) for
evening. With Jouvin gloves costing what they did,
this was serious.

No one is surprised to learn that the novel's central character,
Elie, has run up an enormous 30,000-franc bill at the famous
glove-maker's, but the narrator points out that if Elie had really
been a regular frequenter of the Paris salons over a twenty-year
period, as he claimed, he would have needed between 12,000
and 14,000 pairs of gloves at four francs a pair, proving that
there must have been long gaps in his sorties into high society.
Betrayed by his glove bill, Elie is indeed less well-off and less
well connected than he pretends.[53]

Yet a plentiful supply of fresh, well-fitting gloves in appropriate colours was still not enough to ensure that a hand conveyed
the right message. The gesture of pulling on a glove was also significant, and required meticulous attention. Routledge greatly
admired the care with which French women selected and drew
on their gloves – care sadly lacking in their English counterparts,
who failed to appreciate the wider meanings communicated by
such attention to detail:

> Good, well-fitting gloves and shoes tell more
> than most other things among the French . . .
> It is remarkable that there is nothing which
> distinguishes a foreigner from an Englishwoman
> more than her gloves. They 'fit like a glove'; they
> are of a good colour, according well with the rest
> of the costume, neither too light nor too dark, but
> rather light than dark. There are no ends or corners
> of the fingers which are not well filled; there are no

creases indicative of the gloves being of a wrong size, nor are they put on crooked with a twist given to the fingers, so that the seams of the glove do not appear straight. In short, a Frenchwoman does not put on her glove anyhow as an Englishwoman does. To her it is a matter of great importance; to our country-woman it is a matter of indifference. We think the Frenchwoman right, because it is by what are called trifles that good and also great effects are produced.[54]

Warning his French readers that 'a glove that has been put on badly can only be compared to a jacket with holes at the elbows,' Guenot-Lecointe offered detailed instructions:

So, you take your glove and fold it in two, doubling over on itself the part that is to cover the back of the hand; then you insert your four fingers into the corresponding finger holes of the glove, and, pushing all the way down to the palm with the other hand, you slide them in, taking care not to leave the slightest wrinkle, for wrinkles will stay there and seriously mar the sheen of the leather. Once the four fingers have been thus inserted, it is the turn of the thumb, which you slide in with the same precautions; then you smooth down the fingers and thumb one last time, so that the shape of all your nails is visible. All that remains is to bring down over the hand the part of the glove that you folded back to begin with; the glove is on – now button it up.[55]

But the question of where and when to button up the glove presented more problems. Gloves had to be put on properly before the wearer left the house – 'You should no more be seen pulling on your gloves in the street than tying the strings of your bonnet,' reprimanded one English etiquette manual.[56] And a French author described how a family nearly miss their train because the daughter, fresh from convent school, refuses to leave home before doing up every last glove-button.[57]

More problematic still was the question of when to remove one's gloves. Judging by the frequency with which advice manuals addressed the issue, it was a source of much social anxiety. The rules were neither straightforward nor always the same for men and women, but to transgress them was to betray a lack of breeding. In exceptional cases the removal of a glove could be a display in itself, as the virtuoso pianist Franz Liszt well knew. On the concert platform he would ceremoniously remove his white gloves and toss them on the floor to thunderous applause before his famous hands touched the keys. It was part of the performance, and his discarded gloves gained such iconic status that admirers fought over them.[58] More usually, however, glove-wearers were faced with uncertainty, despite the manuals' attempts to issue clear-cut regulations: 'Never dance without gloves. This is an imperative rule'; 'Gloves should be worn by ladies in church, and in places of public amusement. Do not take them off to shake hands'; 'In the house . . . the rule is imperative, [a gentleman] must not offer a lady a gloved hand.'[59]

In many circumstances multiple calculations – instinctive to those born into glove-wearing society – needed to be made quickly in order not to transmit the wrong signals. Men had to take into account not only the gender and status of the person they were about to greet, but even the weather conditions and the colour of their gloves. Moreover, advice manuals did not always agree, particularly about the delicate matter of glove-to-skin or skin-to-skin hand contact when meeting an acquaintance in the street. *The Gentlemen's Book of Etiquette* gave American readers the following guidance:

George
Washington
Lambert, *Lotty
and a Lady*, 1906,
oil on canvas.
Although the
women hold their
hands in similar
positions, the
lady's spotless
white gloves
emphasize the
social divide
between her and
the maid, whose
bare, reddened
hands handle fish.

In the street, etiquette does not require a gentleman
to take off his glove to shake hands with a lady,
unless her hand is uncovered . . . In the street, if
his hand be very warm or very cold, or the glove
cannot be readily removed, it is much better to offer
the covered hand than to offend the lady's touch,
or delay the salutation during an awkward fumble
to remove the glove.[60]

How to Behave, however, told them that 'Foreigners are sometimes very sensitive in this matter, and might deem the glove
an insult.'[61] Yet *Martine's Hand-book of Etiquette* (1866) said
that:

If it is warm weather it is more agreeable to both parties
that the glove should be on – especially if it is a lady
with whom you shake hands, as the perspiration of
your bare hand would be very likely to soil her glove.[62]

Henry Lunettes went a step further, insisting that 'to touch the
pure glove of a lady with uncovered fingers is – impertinent.'[63]
But there was also a risk that dye from a gentleman's gloved
handshake might contaminate the lady's 'pure glove', and *How
to Behave* recommended that 'If your glove be dark coloured . . .
do not offer to shake hands with a lady in full dress.'[64]

Equally conflicting advice was issued about whether to wear
gloves when eating. The practice is depicted as normal in Balzac's
1830 short story 'Étude de moeurs par les gants' (A Study of
Manners by Means of Gloves). There, a man's claim that an
upset stomach prevented him from dancing at an aristocratic
ball is disproved when his gloves are inspected, for they bear
liqueur stains and traces of food that still smell of vanilla and
pistachio, revealing that he was absent from the dance floor not
because of illness but because he preferred eating to dancing.
The Gentlemen's Book of Etiquette assumes that its readers
wear gloves when eating at dances, and advises men to carry two
pairs:

In handling refreshments, you may soil the pair you
wear on entering the room, and will thus be under the
necessity of offering your hand covered by a soiled
glove, to some fair partner. You can slip unperceived
from the room, change the soiled for a fresh pair, and
then avoid that mortification.[65]

Martine's Hand-book of Etiquette was categorical in its
condemnation of those who ate in gloves, however: 'Neither
ladies nor gentlemen ever wear gloves at table, unless their

hands, from some cause, are not fit to be seen.'⁶⁶ *How to Behave* agreed, telling its readers that 'Nothing is more preposterous than to eat in gloves,' and warning them of the social implications of so doing: 'Snobs sometimes wear gloves at table. It is not necessary that you should imitate them.'⁶⁷ Another American manual commented that having greasy fingers from eating buttered bread or toast 'is of less consequence, now that the absurd practice of eating in gloves is wisely abolished among genteel people'.⁶⁸

Whether they approved of the practice or not, etiquette manuals agreed that eating in gloves was a topic that needed to be addressed. *Manners and Rules of Good Society by a Member of the Aristocracy* advised women to remove their gloves as soon as they sat down at table. It conceded that 'occasionally long elbow gloves are not removed during dinner', but added that 'this is conspicuous and inconvenient.' At wedding luncheons, however, women might keep gloves on, but men should remove theirs.⁶⁹ *The Habits of Good Society* recommended retention: 'As to gloves at tea-parties and so forth, we are generally safer with than without them.'⁷⁰ Mary Cassatt's 1880 painting *The Tea* shows a visitor holding her cup and saucer in elegantly gloved hands while the hostess is appropriately barehanded in her own home.

Such inconsistent advice is possibly explained by gloves' increasingly close fit and the difficulty of removing or rebuttoning long versions in order to eat. This was a problem for which an Englishwoman named Helena Maud Conrad proposed what she considered a practical solution. Applying in 1894 for a patent for her invention, she explained:

> If ladies, when making calls at friends' houses, partake
> of afternoon tea, they generally find it necessary to
> remove the right-hand glove in order to prevent it from
> getting soiled by the buttered bread or other things

that they eat. Now the object of my invention is to obviate this inconvenience by providing a protecting device to be temporarily worn upon the forefinger and thumb over the glove.[71]

Mary Cassatt, *The Tea*, c. 1880, oil on canvas. The visitor wears long gloves while her hostess goes barehanded at home. The etiquette of whether to wear gloves when eating or drinking was much debated.

Whereas Conrad was trying to solve a practical problem, advice manuals presented their guidance about eating in gloves in terms of propriety rather than practicality. The vehemence of their language shows how freighted with social meaning glove-wearing had become. Even in the short extracts quoted here, highly emotive, moralizing terms abound – *mortification, offend, insult, impertinent, preposterous, absurd* – evidence of just how unfortunately eloquent 'wrongly worn' gloves could be.

That eloquence was appreciated by novelists, who realized that gloves could pinpoint a character's social station. Although gloves had been mentioned in literature before the nineteenth century, their fictional presence soared along with the massive expansion in production and glove-wearing in the 1830s and '40s, as writers came to understand, like Marennes, that 'nowadays [gloves] play an important, symbolic role.'[72]

Like the evening gloves that society ladies placed in their wine glasses to tell servants that they did not want alcohol, gloves could quietly communicate meaning. In a novel, the frustrating process of buttoning a tight glove could express the urgency of modern life; characters picking up their gloves signalled that a visit was at an end; and ill-breeding could be revealed by a glove splitting when too large a hand was forced into it. For characters sensitive to society's demands but unable to meet them, gloves are often a source of shame or embarrassment. In Flaubert's *Sentimental Education* (1869), for example, the hero ensures that he is always 'irreproachably gloved' when calling on his beloved Madame Arnoux, but when he can no longer afford decent gloves after losing his inheritance, he fears that he may never see her again: 'He could not turn up wearing shabby black gloves that had gone blue at the fingertips . . . No, no! Never!'[73]

The blatant transgression of glove-wearing rules could be equally telling, and characters such as the opera singer in James Joyce's *Dubliners* (1914), who 'marred the good impression by wiping his nose in his gloved hand once or twice out of thoughtlessness', are neatly pigeonholed by their behaviour.[74] Revealing the gap between how individuals treated their gloves and the rules of polite society was a succinct way of delineating character and class.

Gloves' communicative power often helps to propel a narrative. When Charles Dickens writes that Mr Vholes, the morally bankrupt lawyer in *Bleak House* (1852), 'takes off his close black gloves as if he were skinning his hands', the reader immediately senses this is not someone to be trusted.[75] Equally telling are the frequent references to gloves in Thomas Hardy's *Tess of the d'Urbervilles* (1891), whose plot development they foreshadow. The mismatch between Alec d'Urberville and Tess is signalled by the contrast between his elegant brown driving gloves and the stout leather gauntlets that Tess, like her fellow workers in the fields, wears to protect her hands from sharp stubble. When d'Urberville suddenly turns to take Tess's hand, the text's focus on her glove reveals that although, like *The Heptameron*'s English lord, he manages to capture the glove, the girl, like her hand, will elude him:

> the buff-glove was on it, and he seized only the rough leather fingers which did not express the life or shape of those within.
> 'You must not – you must not!' she cried fearfully, slipping her hand from the glove as from a pocket, and leaving it in his grasp.[76]

Later, when Tess is pushed to the limit by d'Urberville, the violent blow struck by her glove prefigures the knife attack that will eventually kill him:

> without the slightest warning she passionately swung the glove by the gauntlet directly in his face. It was heavy and thick as a warrior's, and it struck him flat on the mouth . . . and in a moment the blood began dropping from his mouth upon the straw.[77]

But gloves' ability to express character or social status or to foreshadow action is not the only reason why novelists and playwrights find them useful. Gloves can provide clues or shed light on mysteries, and for that reason often feature in detective fiction. Several of Sherlock Holmes's ingenious deductions are based on information divulged by the quality of a glove's leather, its scuff marks, its appropriateness. And in *Mrs Halliburton's Troubles*, Mrs Halliburton's son is proved innocent after being wrongly suspected of passing a stolen cheque when it turns out that the only pair of gloves he possesses is black, whereas the culprit was known to have had 'Clean light gloves . . . such as gentlemen wear'.[78]

If gloves can prove innocence or identify a criminal, they are equally capable of being misread and complicating the solving of a crime. In 'The Pair of Gloves', the second of Dickens's *Three Detective Anecdotes* (1850), a pair of men's gloves is discovered in the bed of a young woman whose throat has been cut. The gloves are presented as a crucial clue to the identity of the murderer, but when elaborate detective work finally traces their owner there turns out to be an innocent explanation for their presence in the bed. Their owner had no connection with the crime.

Similarly misleading is the 'long ladies' glove of Danish leather, delicately worked and brand new, but soiled with dark spots that the doctor recognized as blood', which is found hanging from a bush near the body of a man who has clearly met a violent end in Otto Ludwig's novella *The Dead Man of St Anne's Chapel* (1839).[79] There, too, the glove is presented as a significant clue. As the victim's brother says: 'We're beginning to see the light! . . . The glove is an important piece of evidence. It's clear that the wounded lady lost it; it's for the right hand. We'll also find that hand!'[80]

The hand of the initial suspect proves too big for the glove, but when a matching left glove is found, its owner is traced and sent for trial. In court, however, the defence lawyer reads a different story from the gloves. Seeking to cast doubt on the identification between glove and individual, he argues that since thousands of similar gloves have been sold, the two displayed as evidence are not necessarily a pair. He also points out that the bloodstained glove was not necessarily dropped at the time of the crime, or by the woman accused. In a final twist we discover that although the gloves are indeed a pair, and do belong to the suspect, she is innocent. There was no murder – the dead man had committed suicide.

Such tales see gloves as eloquent witnesses that can incriminate or vindicate, but whose evidence may be hard to interpret. They can testify in real life, too, as in the infamous 1994 trial of O. J. Simpson, where a left-hand glove found at the scene of his ex-wife's murder became a much-disputed piece of evidence, interpreted by prosecution and defence in very different ways. ('If it doesn't fit, you must acquit,' argued Simpson's lawyer.) As that trial showed, the messages that gloves transmit can be as flexible and ambiguous as the accessories themselves.

Eloquent though gloves might be, Flaubert saw them differently. For him they represented the stifling of expression. Although alert to their metaphorical potential, he believed that they withheld meaning rather than communicating it. Tight gloves were associated in his mind with the constraints and falsity of bourgeois culture, and he dismissed as 'barbarism in white gloves' what he saw as the airless literature of his contemporaries.[81] Gloves blunted creativity, he argued, and he compared the way they constricted the hands to the constraints that language imposed on the literary imagination.[82] Great ideas straining against the limitations of language were, he said, like a big hand bursting through the seams of an overtight glove.[83] He tried to explain his reaction in a note headed *Théorie du gant* (Theory of the Glove):

> It idealizes the hand by depriving it of its colour, just as rice flour does for the face; it makes it inexpressive (think of the unpleasant effect that gloves have on stage), but typical; only the shape is preserved and accentuated. That artificial colour, grey, white or yellow, blends in with the sleeve of the costume and [without] conveying the idea of something different (since the outline is preserved), introduces novelty

into the known, and so makes this covered member resemble the limb of a statue. And yet this anti-natural thing can move (in this it differs from a mask, though a mask does have movement through the eyes). There is nothing more disturbing than a gloved hand.[84]

Above all, Flaubert was sensitive to the unsettling, uncanny quality of the glove, simultaneously so like and so unlike a hand. That sense of gloves as strangely troubling, enigmatic objects would later be shared by the Surrealists, in whose work a glove often features as a cryptic presence, seemingly significant but unexplained. For them, the language of gloves was mysteriously, and satisfyingly, elusive.

Deg Hit'an gloves of caribou leather and wolfskin with decorative stitching.
Such gloves were worn for distributing gifts at a potlatch; the spirit of the
gifts was believed to remain with the gloves, attracting future wealth and
prestige to their owner.

FOUR

'Fashioned by the Craft of Devils, and with Skins of the Dragon': Magical Gloves

Glove manufacturers, eager to persuade clients of the transformative effects of their merchandise, have often claimed magical qualities for them. 'Wonder-fabric Crescendoe gloves magically slim your hands, wash and wear endlessly, never shrink,' announced one American advertisement in 1954, while the Dawnelle glove company gave its styles names such as 'Black Magic', 'White Magic' and 'Color Magic'.[1] A long-running series of advertisements for Underwood typewriters, from the 1950s, ran with the idea and featured a pair of long, golden gloves which typed by themselves while a secretary looked on in wonderment; the slogan was 'Golden touch typing – like wearing "Magic Gloves".' Today, beauticians can buy 'Portable Gentle Magic Gloves with Microcurrent Technology' that promise to magically transform clients' wrinkles and double chins by emitting tiny electrical impulses.[2] But overexcited copywriters are not alone in attributing supernatural qualities to gloves. Where Flaubert saw them as strangely unsettling and enigmatic, over the centuries others have sensed in them a mystical quality that is reflected in the many myths, legends and superstitions that tell of gloves possessed of mysterious powers.

Like Crescendoe's 'Wonder-fabric' gloves, gloves credited with supernatural properties are often represented as deriving their magical power from the outlandish materials of which

they are made. The great Renaissance humanist and satirist
François Rabelais tells the reader that the vast gloves of his
giant, Gargantua, were sewn from the skins of sixteen goblins
and trimmed with the fur of three werewolves. In popular belief
these creatures were indestructible, a quality that the gloves
surely confer on Gargantua.[3] (That supposedly invulnerable
beings were skinned to make them is a typically Rabelaisian

Wide flared cuffs of shining black Stehli satin.
Double-woven cotton...caressingly smooth,
wonderfully rich. A simply elegant glove!
Ask for BLACK MAGIC...$7.50.

dawnelle

MADE MARK

MANNE & WEILL, INC. • New York • Kansas City • San Francisco

YOUR FAVORITE STORE MAY HAVE OTHER DAWNELLE GLOVE STYLES IF THE ONE ILLUSTRATED IS NOT AVAILABLE.

Advertisement
for Dawnelle's
'Black Magic'
gloves. Post-war
advertising
often claimed
'magical'
qualities for
their gloves.

One of a
series of 1950s
advertisements
for Underwood
typewriters
that feature
autonomous
golden 'Magic
Gloves' to convey
the ease of the
product's 'Golden
Touch Typing'.

tease.) Dragon-hide gloves afford similarly miraculous protection to characters ranging from J. K. Rowling's Harry Potter and
his classmates to the monstrous Grendel of the Anglo-Saxon
epic poem *Beowulf*, whose 'ample and wondrous glove hung
fast by cunning bands . . . [and] was cunningly fashioned by the
craft of devils, and with skins of the dragon'.[4] Although crafted
from a more mundane substance than dragon-skin, the iron
gloves of the Norse god Thor defy that metal's rigidity and con-
ductivity, and magically enable him to catch and deflect red-hot
projectiles. Regardless of their material, however, supernatural
gloves almost always provide total, miraculous protection for the
wearer. If Grendel's massive dragon-skin glove ultimately fails
to prevent his hand and arm from being ripped off as he fights

with Beowulf, its inability to save him only serves to demonstrate Beowulf's extraordinary superhuman strength.

On one level, there is little difference between gloves credited with magical properties and the everyday variety. Like ordinary gloves that shield the hands from heat, cold, dirt or injury, magical gloves form a protective barrier between the wearer and the outside world. And just as ordinary gloves are sometimes used to prevent the outward transfer of contamination from the hands that wear them, so magical gloves at times function to protect the outside world from a danger within. In the Disney film *Frozen* (2013), the slim blue-green glove worn by the young Snow Queen, Elsa, is able to contain her hand's magic powers and prevent them from being unleashed to turn everything around to snow and ice. The difference from ordinary gloves is one of scale, for those represented as magical can avert a threat that is exceptional and extreme; the protective barrier they provide is impenetrable.

That supernatural barrier often denotes the distinction between good and evil. In 'Faithful John', a tale by the Brothers Grimm, evil is magically deflected by what are apparently ordinary gloves. The story tells of a loyal retainer who repeatedly saves the lives of a young king and his bride after overhearing ravens discussing the dangers that lie in wait for the royal couple. At one point the king is about to put on a shimmering wedding shirt that appears to have been woven from gold and silver, but is in fact a magically poisoned garment of sulphur and pitch, designed to burn him to the bone if he wears it. Thanks to the talking ravens, Faithful John knows that the only remedy is for him to seize the shirt in gloved hands and throw it into the fire before the king can touch it, and this he does. Although Faithful John's gloves protect him from the dark magic of the shirt, the gloves themselves are not represented as supernatural. Rather, their function in the tale is to mark the boundary between John's selfless loyalty and an external evil that threatens the king, so demonstrating the triumph of John's exemplary altruism and the vanquishing of malevolent powers. Thanks to the gloves, evil is defeated.

The capacity of gloves to shield the hands from external harm doubtless explains why they have often been credited with providing supernatural protection from dangers both physical and spiritual. A remarkable number of folktales associate gloves with moral virtue. The popular *vantevän* or 'glove-friend' legend, found in several versions along the coastal areas of northern Europe, features a strange creature that emerges from stormy seas and reaches out her hands to a nearby fishing boat, wailing 'I'm so cold, I'm so cold!' When the boat's skipper throws her a pair of gloves, she calls him her 'glove-friend' and tells him to steer for the eastern shore, so saving the boat from being dashed to pieces in the storm.[5] Freely given by the skipper with no expectation of recompense, the gloves in this tale represent a generous and humane gesture. As in the story of Faithful John, their status hovers between the mundane and the supernatural: what were ordinary fisherman's gloves take on new import when given to the merwoman, and the irrationality of a sea creature needing warm gloves only adds to their mystery. The selfless gift of gloves becomes a miraculously beneficial transaction that saves skipper, boat and crew.

Given their apparent ability to mediate between human and mystical spheres, and between good and evil, it is unsurprising that miraculous gloves should appear in accounts of saints' lives and Christian phenomena. Although the physical appearance of such gloves is rarely described, in one case they were evidently costly and fashionable. Lady Eleanor Davies, incarcerated in 1633 for her apocalyptic prophesies, claimed to have been visited in prison by an angel wearing an amber glove on his right hand. The heavenly being blessed her with the gloved hand before vanishing, leaving behind only 'an odiferous scent'. According to Lady Eleanor, the lingering perfume emanated from the glove, which was 'all oyled with Ambergreece, the spirit thereof proceeding from the Leather, so far beyond expression as if it were invisible food'.[6] For Lady Eleanor, the exquisite scent left behind by the angel's glove was proof of her heavenly visitation: spanning the spiritual and the secular, the perfumed glove was both a guarantee that she had been blessed by a divine presence, and reassuring evidence that the angel followed upper-class fashion.

The glove involved in a miracle attributed to Bishop Poppo was of a very different kind but, like the angel's glove, it served as proof of the divine. It is said that in the tenth century, having had little success in bringing Christianity to the people of Jutland, Poppo ordered an iron glove to be made and heated until it was white-hot. After wearing the burning glove 'for a reasonable time', he removed it and displayed his miraculously unscathed hand, a feat of wonder that caused the Danes to embrace the new religion.[7]

Miraculous gloves also feature in the life of the Anglo-Saxon St Audrey, where again they are credited with converting a sinner to the path of righteousness. Abused and berated by her angry husband, Audrey is said to have listened patiently before removing her gloves and flinging them down in front of him. But instead of falling to the ground, the gloves remained suspended in mid-air, hanging motionless on a sunbeam, and on witnessing this miracle the husband saw the error of his ways and begged forgiveness. Miraculously gravity-defying gloves are again associated with St Gudula, the patron saint of Brussels. When a kindly priest found her praying barefoot in church, he placed his gloves under her feet to make her more comfortable. But disdaining comfort, Gudula threw them aside, and like the gloves of St Audrey, they hung motionless in the air for an hour. Poised mid-air like a priest's outstretched hands in the *orans* posture of prayer, the miraculous gloves of such tales are objects of wonder and reverence for all who witness them. Representing a bridge

between earth and heaven, they imply a pure communion with
the divine.

Gloves also feature in the life of St Columban, on whose
shoulders birds and squirrels allegedly rode as he walked through
the woods. One day he is said to have left his gloves outside on
a stone while he went indoors to eat, and he returned to find
that one glove had disappeared. The thief was sought, but St
Columban knew that only a raven, the bird that failed to return
to Noah's ark, would have dared to take it, and he warned that
the raven would be unable to feed its young unless it restored
the glove. The bird immediately flew down with the stolen glove
and waited to be punished, but instead it received the saint's
forgiveness. Here again, a glove mediates between saint and
sinner, and as in the tale of St Audrey, the incident ends in com-
passion and forgiveness, key attributes of Christian saints and,
by extension, their gloves.

Because of their intimate contact with the hand, the gloves
of saints are felt not only to retain the spiritual essence of their
owners but, like them, to be capable of performing miracles.
The fraudulent Pardoner in Chaucer's *Canterbury Tales* is able
to exploit this belief when he produces a mitten and assures his
pious audience that – if they pay him – it will bring them riches:

'Now look; I have a mitten here, a glove.
Whoever wears this mitten on his hand
Will multiply his grain. He sows his land
And up will come abundant wheat or oats,
Providing that he offers pence or groats.'[8]

Like the twelfth-century gloves of St Thomas à Becket, credited with miraculous healing and venerated by pilgrims to his
shrine, saints' gloves continue to inspire the faithful with their
holy powers. In twenty-first-century America, the shrine of the
recently canonized St Gianna Beretta Molla attracts women

hoping to conceive, who come to touch and venerate the saint's gloves as they ask for her intercession. The black leather gloves were donated to the church by the saint's husband on condition that the faithful be allowed direct physical contact with them, and pilgrims are also given prayer cards that have touched the gloves in a further dissemination of their saintly influence.[9]

Mystical powers attributed to gloves are not always benevolent, however. Just as saints' gloves are credited with delivering saintly actions, so the gloves of evildoers are reputed to produce evil. Filmmakers recognize this when they convey the sinister malice of a villain by showing a close-up of his black-gloved hand. It comes as no surprise that the creators of the American comic-book superhero Batman should have given the name 'Black Glove' to the diabolical organization that is determined to destroy him and everything he stands for, or that when the sexton in Nathaniel Hawthorne's *The Scarlet Letter* (1850) finds a black glove lying 'on the scaffold where evil-doers are set up to public shame', he should conclude that 'Satan dropped it there.'[10]

Even when detached from the hand, the gloves of evildoers are often believed to share the owner's depraved nature and malevolent power. Among the tales collected by Walter Scott in *Minstrelsy of the Scottish Border* (1802) is one that demonstrates evil transferred from owner to glove. The story tells of a young prince who repulses the advances of his wicked stepmother, a 'witch-lady'. Furious at being rejected, she strikes him with her wolfskin glove and curses him, turning him into a huge bear who is doomed to live in the woods, devour the king's herds and eventually be killed and eaten in his turn.[11] In this tale not only does the wolfskin glove embody the evil savagery of the witch-stepmother, but its touch effectively transmits that savagery to her victim, condemning him to live like a beast and prey on animals as a wolf would do.

In these examples, the relationship between hand and glove is closer than ever. Even apart, the two seem inseparable, sharing the same attributes and wielding the same power. Characteristic of that magically porous borderline between hand and glove, good and evil, human and beast, is Hans Christian Andersen's tale of 'The Marsh King's Daughter', in which, as in so many fairy tales, a beautiful girl has been turned into a frog. When a priest is murdered, the frog-maiden performs an act of Christian mercy by burying his body and drawing the sign of the cross on his grave with her two webbed 'hands'. As she does so, 'the web skin fell away from her fingers like a torn glove. She washed her hands at the spring and gazed in astonishment at their delicate whiteness.'[12] Neither hand-shaped nor webbed, yet fitting both a frog's foreleg and a human hand, the 'torn glove' of skin in this tale hovers between the girl's accursed bestial state and her new-found humanity, until water symbolically purifies and restores her hand as a consequence of her charitable action.

Even more emblematic of those blurred boundaries are gloves featured in the *Völsunga* saga, an Icelandic myth about the three sons of Sigmund. The boys' mother sews gloves to their hands, driving her needle through glove, skin and flesh. Two of her sons scream in agony, but the third boy, Sinfjotli, makes no complaint even when the gloves are ripped off his hands, taking his skin with them. He thus proves himself a true member of the Völsung clan.[13] As in 'The Marsh King's Daughter', the glove and the skin of the hand are as one, and their removal marks a transformative revelation – of the frog-maiden's true human form in one case, and of the third son's supernatural power in the other.

In all these tales, gloves hold a delicate balance between the normal and the paranormal. Conjurers understand this when they don white gloves to perform their stage magic, for gloves have long been seen as helping to navigate between the real world and the realm of the supernatural, between the familiar and the strange or, in the case of saints' gloves, between the secular and the divine. The cartoonists who devised the figure of Mickey Mouse made good use of that capacity to bridge two

Conjurers' stage mystique is enhanced by the white gloves they conventionally wear to perform.

realms. As Walt Disney explained: 'We didn't want him to have mouse hands, because he was supposed to be more human. So we gave him gloves.'[14] Mickey Mouse's gloves are not quite those of a human, though. The fact that they have only four digits demonstrates that he is neither a man nor a mouse, but something strangely in between.

The role of gloves in representing that mysterious shifting between dimensions is particularly evident in the long, ceremonial sealskin mittens covered with puffins' beaks that men of the Inupiat community in Alaska wear to perform the traditional Eagle-Wolf dance. The ritual enables the spirits of creatures killed by hunters to return to the spirit world to be reborn, and part of the dance enacts the transformation of swallows into wolves. Rattling with beaks and entirely covering the dancers' arms, perhaps in imitation of swallows' wings, the sealskin mittens are an essential component in a ritual performance of killing and regeneration, where distinctions between humans, birds and animals dissolve along with the division between life and death.[15]

In all these instances, the borderline between hand and glove, between human and animal or between the living and the lifeless is fluid. Questions of agency consequently become blurred and troubling. Who or what controls these uncanny gloves? Often, gloves are credited with the mysterious ability to act independently of any hand, like the golden gloves that type by themselves in the Underwood advertisements, or the pair of empty leather gloves that twiddle their thumbs in Harry Potter's Ministry of Magic.[16] Similarly the magic glove in Jean Cocteau's 1946 film *La Belle et la bête* (Beauty and the Beast) transports Beauty between the Beast's castle and her father's home in the twinkling of an eye. Gloves' supernatural ability to function without human agency is equally evident in many popular superstitions, where they appear as repositories of good or bad fortune, or as channels for fate:

> It is unlucky to roll your gloves together; you roll up your luck. Dropping the left glove is a sign that your lover is thinking of you. To find a pair of gloves is . . . a sign of a wedding, particularly your own. If you put your glove on the wrong hand, it is a sign that you will hear from absent friends. To rip a glove while stretching it, is a sign that someone is trying to do you evil. It is ill luck to put on any other person's gloves, as it will sever friendship.[17]

Inupiat drawing from the 1890s, showing Inupiat men wearing long mittens covered with puffin beaks to perform the ritual Eagle-Wolf dance.

If strange powers were thought to adhere to gloves, then putting on a glove that was not one's own – inserting one's hands into someone else's identity – was seen as potentially dangerous. A tale recorded in fourteenth-century Ireland warns of dreadful consequences:

> In the County of Leinster, there happened such
> a strange prodigy as had never been heard of.
> A person, travelling along the road, found a pair
> of gloves fit for his hands, as he thought; but when
> he put them on, he lost his speech immediately, and
> could do nothing but bark like a dog; nay, from
> that moment, the men and women, old and young,
> throughout the whole country, barked like dogs, and
> the children like whelps. This plague continued with
> some 18 days, with others a month, and with some
> for two years, and, like a contagious distemper, at
> last infected the neighbouring counties, and set them
> a barking too.[18]

Rattling beaks cover these ritual dance mittens from the Aleutian Islands, Alaska.

A still from Jean
Cocteau's *Beauty
and the Beast*
(1946), showing
Beauty wearing a
magic glove that
can transport
her wherever she
wishes.

While readers today might dismiss this as an account of a whooping cough epidemic which happened to coincide with someone finding a pair of lost gloves, it is clear that contemporaries saw it as a cautionary tale which reinforced a fear that gloves were capable of unleashing malevolent forces and turning humans into beasts. Such glove-related superstitions were widespread. A few, such as the warning commonly expressed in the nineteenth century that it was unlucky to wear gloves in the house or to put gloves on in the street, seem designed to encourage compliance with prevailing etiquette; more often, however, they imply belief in a mysterious connection between a glove and some powerful, unseen, cosmic agency.

Such beliefs are visible in the designs hand-knitted into traditional Latvian mittens which incorporate magic symbols – sun and star signs, crosses of the goddess Māra and symbols of Zalktis, the sacred snake – into their woollen patterns to protect the wearer from evil. Even gloves that have no wearer have been credited with the power to ward off bad luck. London's Horniman Museum owns a fine example of an amuletic glove: a brown leather glove with white stitching has been bound at the

Protective magic symbols are incorporated into the designs of traditional Latvian knitted mittens.

wrist and stuffed with pink wool to make it resemble a gloved hand whose fingers form the *mano cornuta* gesture – the sign of the horns – to ward off the Evil Eye.

Belief in gloves' mysterious interaction with good and evil has been represented in many different ways. Some magically reveal the truth; others conceal iniquity. In one of the Arthurian legends, for example, a hostile fairy named Giramphiel sends a glove with revelatory properties to the king's court, where it is passed round all the courtiers. When they put it on, they become invisible except for the parts of their body that have sinned. The glove shames everyone except Arthur and his nephew Gawain, the only two to pass this test of virtue.[19]

By showing how wrongdoing is exposed by Giramphiel's magic glove, the legend extends gloves' old association with honesty and rectitude into the realm of the supernatural. Conversely, everyday worries that gloves may conceal something ugly or fraudulent also find supernatural expression. Many tales feature a diabolical figure which disguises its true nature by hiding its scaly claws inside gloves, and generations of children may have become wary of glove-wearing adults after reading Roald Dahl's description of witches:

a REAL WITCH is certain always to be wearing gloves
when you meet her . . . Because she doesn't have
finger-nails. Instead of finger-nails, she has thin
curvy claws, like a cat, and she wears the gloves
to hide them . . . Witches wear gloves even in the
house. They only take them off to go to bed.[20]

Equally disturbing are gloves that act alone, with no hand
inside. Although the empty gloves that speed-type in Underwood's
advertisements or twiddle their thumbs in the Harry Potter
books are harmlessly intriguing – an eye-catching way of imply-
ing ease of use in the one case, and a quirky detail contributing
to the novel's atmosphere of enchantment in the other –
independently active gloves are often less innocuous. Elizabeth
Bowen's short story 'Hand in Glove' (1952) is a chilling tale of
empty gloves unleashing dark forces as they pursue their malign
intent. Ethel and Elsie, two impoverished but socially ambitious
sisters, live with a bedridden aunt whom they maltreat, and
whose trunks filled with clothes from her once glamorous life
they secretly plunder for their needs. There is, however, one thing
that they are unable to source from the trunks:

All that they were short of was evening gloves – they
had two pairs each, which they had been compelled to

A glove amulet,
stuffed with pink
wool to resemble
a hand making
the *mano cornuto*
gesture to ward
off bad luck.
Europe, late
19th or early
20th century.

buy. *What* could have become of Mrs Varley de Grey's presumably sumptuous numbers of this item, they were unable to fathom, and it was too bad.[21]

The sisters are obliged to clean their own meagre glove supply every evening with benzene, and its penetrating smell pursues them as they whirl around the ballroom floor, repulsing an English lord whom Ethel had resolved to marry. When she tries to prise open the final, locked trunk in her determination to find her aunt's store of gloves, 'the spotless finger-tip of a white kid glove appeared for a moment, as though exploring its way out, then withdrew,' and the trunk bursts open of its own accord:

> She should have fled. But oh, how she craved what
> lay there exposed! – layer upon layer, wrapped in
> transparent paper, of elbow-length, magnolia-pure
> white gloves, bedded on the inert folds of the veil
> . . . Ethel flung herself forward on to that sea of kid,
> scrabbling and seizing. The glove she had seen before
> was now, however, readier for its purpose. At first it
> merely pounced after Ethel's fingers, as though making
> mock of their greedy course; but the hand within it
> was all the time filling out . . . With one snowy flash
> through the dusk, the glove clutched Ethel's front
> hair, tangled itself in her black curls and dragged her
> head down. She began to choke among the sachets
> and tissue – then the glove let go, hurled her back, and
> made its leap at her throat.
>
> It was a marvel that anything so dainty should be
> so strong. So great, so convulsive was the swell of the
> force that, during the strangling of Ethel, the seams of
> the glove split.
>
> In any case, the glove would have been too small
> for her.[22]

The combination of everyday detail (the dainty glove is the wrong size for Ethel and its seams give way under pressure) with supernatural violence adds to the uncanny impact of the gloves as they enact the vengeful rage of their absent, dying owner. These gloves present a moral counterpart to the pair in the tale of the sea creature who complained of the cold. Whereas in the folktale warm gloves were freely given in an act of charity that was rewarded when the crew's lives were saved, Bowen's story is one of selfishness and greed rather than open-handed exchange. Her autonomous gloves punish rather than reward, acting as a proxy for their owner as they ruthlessly carry out the aunt's last wishes.

The troubling sense that gloves are capable of independent action takes a different form in Stanley Kubrick's film *Dr Strangelove* (1964). Rather than acting on behalf of its owner, the single black glove that the doctor wears on his right hand is violently at odds with him. It fights to control his hand movements, forces him to make a Nazi salute and tries to throttle him in an apparent struggle of wills. The sinister black glove graphically symbolizes Strangelove's malevolent side and his struggle to contain it. Equally malign is the disembodied Dreadful Flying Glove featured in the Beatles' film *The Yellow Submarine* (1968), which swoops through the air like a missile, wraps itself around enemies and rolls itself into a fist to deliver devastating blows. Part destructive weapon, part ferocious beast, the glove is a surreal invention of the 1960s, yet its roots reach back to old fears about gloves' mysterious powers and dangerous agency.

So potent was the perceived connection between a glove and its owner that at one time it was believed that a victim would experience any torture inflicted on his or her glove, however far apart they might be. A stolen glove might be stuffed with wax or herbs or maggots, or stuck through with nails, to torment its owner. Burying the glove of an enemy was thought to cause him or her to waste away as it rotted: gloves could commit murder.

When Joan Flower and her two daughters, former servants at Belvoir Castle in Leicestershire, were accused of killing the Earl of Rutland's heir and put on trial in 1618–19, the women confessed to having stolen, boiled and repeatedly pricked the glove of their intended victim in order to bring about his death. The so-called 'witches of Belvoir' also admitted that they had stolen a pair of gloves from the earl and his wife along with feathers from their bed, and had boiled them with a little blood to prevent the birth of any further heirs.[23]

The sense that a powerful and mysterious bond existed between glove and owner was once widespread, and superstitions warned people against losing both their gloves in case they were found by a witch, who would then have them in her power. The belief has persisted into recent times, as a wax-filled leather glove in the Museum of Witchcraft and Magic in Cornwall, England, confirms. The museum's records explain that in 1979

In Stanley Kubrick's 1964 film *Dr Strangelove*, the doctor's hand movements appear to be controlled against his will by the black glove he wears on one hand.

a Plymouth woman had taken one of her daughter's gloves to a witch and asked her to end the girl's relationship with an unsuitable man, confident that once in possession of the glove, the witch would have control over the daughter.

The flexibility of gloves' supernatural gifts, with their apparent ability to operate between the physical and spiritual worlds, is graphically demonstrated by a class of folktale in which humans who have been led astray by fairies manage to break the magic spell by turning a glove inside out.[24] Reversing the glove, turning its inner surface away from the hand to break that intimate contact, was believed to deflect the magic power.

Such potent flexibility is also reflected in tales where gloves appear to change shape or fluctuate in size. In an Irish folktale retold by W. B. Yeats, for instance, a seemingly harmless old woman is suddenly transformed into a terrifying adversary when she dons 'a pair of boxing-gloves, each one of them nine stone weight, and the nails in them fifteen inches long'.[25] Another improbably huge glove features in the Icelandic *Prose Edda*, where Thor and his companions take refuge for the night in a great chamber leading off an enormous hall, only to discover the next morning that they have been sleeping inside the thumb of a vast glove belonging to the giant Skrymir.[26] Many Nordic troll stories feature incongruously large gloves that serve to emphasize the gigantic stature of an ogre.

In further strangeness, gloves become receptacles for enormous objects or beasts rather than hands. One Nordic story features a troll whose glove is big enough to contain a barrel of rye, and Grendel's dragon-skin glove is capable of coping with the monster's plan of cramming Beowulf and all his men into it. Less disturbingly, a Ukrainian folktale tells how a series of animals lost in the snow creep into a small boy's dropped mitten, which has no difficulty in accommodating the mole, rabbit, hedgehog, owl, badger, fox, bear and fieldmouse that congregate there.

As gloves in tales like these fluctuate between being places of refuge or imprisonment, their unnaturally distorted dimensions convey a world that is unnervingly disorientating. With their inherent flexibility and reversibility, gloves lend themselves to an association with shape-shifting powers. They are ideal, multi-functional symbolic objects, able to slip smoothly between the realms of reality and magical fantasy, promising good luck or ill fortune, protecting or attacking, bringing salvation or death. So while some magic narratives feature gloves voluminous enough to swallow up bands of warriors or groups of animals, others rely on the intimate fit between glove and hand.

Nowhere do close-fitting gloves behave more mysteriously than in the 1950 film *Orphée*, whose director, Jean Cocteau, used surgical gloves and reverse-motion cinematography to create the impression that gloves given to Orpheus were being moulded to his hands by some supernatural force. Exemplary in their ability to glide from one realm into another, taking their wearer with them, these magic gloves allow Orpheus to pass through a mirror from the world of the living into the afterlife.

Elsewhere, magic gloves play a crucial role in exploring issues of identity and kinship. One such pair features in the Middle English romance *Sir Degare*, the strange tale of a knight born in secret to a princess who had been raped by a fairy. Degare is brought up by a hermit and his sister, and when he reaches adulthood they give him a pair of magic gloves, together with a letter revealing that the only hands they will fit are those of his mother. Degare sets off on a quest to find her, unsuccessfully trying the gloves on women he encounters on the way. He eventually comes to the royal court, where the king has decreed that his daughter may only marry a man who can defeat him in a tournament. Degare challenges the king, is declared the victor and is immediately married to the princess. On their wedding night he suddenly remembers the gloves, and when they fit the bride perfectly, the couple realize that they must be mother and son. Like Cinderella's

In Jean Cocteau's 1950 film *Orphée*, magic gloves allow Orpheus to pass through a mirror into the realm of the dead.

Just believe.

slipper, these magic gloves lead Degare to the only person who can wear them. In an inversion of the Cinderella story, however, rather than bringing about a marriage, they dissolve one and so prevent an incestuous union.

Gloves play a related role in a Judeo-Spanish folktale in which a dying wife urges her husband never to remarry unless he finds a woman for whom her own gloves are a perfect fit. The only person they will fit is the couple's young daughter, and it is only by hiding inside a wooden doll that she manages to avoid her father's incestuous intentions.[27] Although the gloves' exclusive fit is designed to deter the husband from remarrying, their dark magic works to encourage incest, rather than averting it as in *Sir Degare*. Symbolic of the husband's misplaced desire, the gloves that fit both wife and daughter merge the identities of the two women, and it is only by guile that the girl escapes their power and her father's advances.

However fantastical the gloves in these tales may seem, all are rooted in some form of lived experience. Despite their apparent strangeness, their magic powers may be seen as intensified or imaginatively distorted versions of reality. The awe and

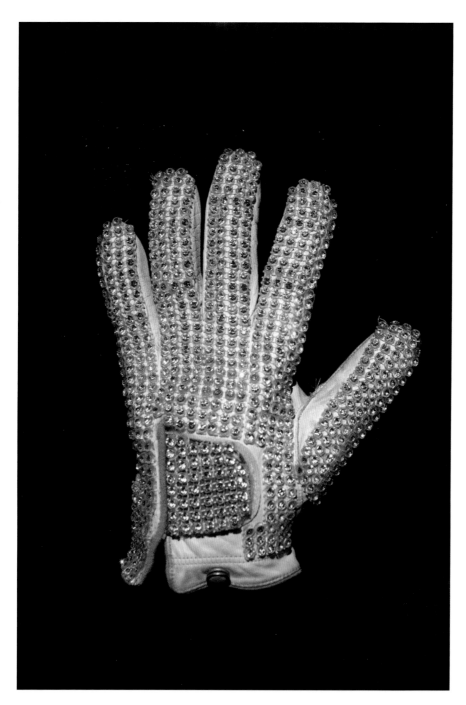

The glove worn by Michael Jackson for his moonwalk dance in 1983.
In 2009 it sold at auction for $350,000.

wonderment provoked in the devout by the gloves of miracle-working saints is perhaps not so different from the excited reverence that the gloves of modern celebrities generate in their fans, who sometimes pay huge sums for them. In 2014 the boxing gloves worn by Muhammad Ali in his first fight against Sonny Liston sold at auction for $836,500. The single glittering, white glove worn by Michael Jackson when he first performed his famous moonwalk dance in 1983 fetched $350,000 some 26 years later, and in a turn of phrase suggestive of miraculous properties, the head of the auction house described it as 'the Holy Grail of Michael Jackson'.[28] Similarly, those dragon- or goblin-skin gloves that offered the wearer miraculous protection were only taking to extremes the protection from heat, cold, dirt or injury afforded by real-life gloves and gauntlets. Gloves that mysteriously act independently of any hand merely extend the convention whereby the glove of a monarch delivered royal authority to distant parts. Beauty's glove, with its magical ability to transport her wherever she wishes, has its equivalent in the richly ornamented gloves of an aristocratic elite whose wealth and rank granted them free access to power and prestige. And gloves that magically inflict terrible punishment or injury, such as the witch-lady's wolfskin glove, or the Dreadful Flying Glove from the Beatles' *Yellow Submarine*, or the Glove of Mynhegon, a fearsome magic gauntlet that featured in the television series *Buffy the Vampire Slayer* (1997–2003), have more mundane counterparts in the many non-magic gloves designed for violence through the ages, from metal-reinforced Roman *caesti* to a lethal gun-glove designed for the u.s. Navy.

Whether or not we try to rationalize the magical powers that have been attributed to gloves over the centuries, the attribution itself is significant. It reflects a persistent sense that, in their ambiguous relationship to hands – eerily shadowing their form and movements, yet separate from the body – gloves are intrinsically mysterious.

Carolus-Duran, *The Lady with the Glove*, 1869, oil on canvas. The
deliberate dropping of a glove was recognized as a seductive invitation.

FIVE

'Place this Glove neere thy Heart': Gloves and Loves

In the tale with which this book began – the story of the English lord who proudly wore a lady's jewel-encrusted glove pinned to his cloak – it is clear that the precious glove functions not only as an emblem of his enduring love for the lady, but as a substitute for it. With the lady beyond his reach, the lord's emotions focus entirely on her fetishized glove, now the object of his devotion. Although the story is an unusual one, the close and curious relationship between glove and love that it explores is echoed in different forms in countless works of literature and art, as well as in traditional customs and folklore. Jean Godard imagined gloves as having been invented by none other than Venus, the goddess of love, and many gloves, particularly in the eighteenth and early nineteenth centuries, were imprinted with images of cupids or embracing lovers.[1] As fashion journalist Clara Young points out, gloves themselves offer a sensual embrace: 'The pleasure of putting on a pair of perfect-fitting gloves, sheathing one's hands in gorgeously supple leather and slowly fitting them over one's fingers . . . appeal[s] to the most primeval tactile needs.'[2]

Gloves belong in pairs. Left- and right-hand gloves are different yet complementary and, like a loving couple, they form a perfect match. The pairing metaphor is clear in twin portraits from 1644 of Joseph Coymans and his wife, Dorothea Berck, by the Dutch artist Frans Hals. Joseph wears a plain white glove on his left hand while Dorothea wears its partner on her right, the matching gloves symbolizing the bond between husband

and wife. A long tradition of lovers being united by a pair of gloves derives from the same analogy, and many superstitions have developed around an association between gloves and court-ship or marriage. It was once believed that hanging a pair of gloves over the church pew of an unmarried individual would induce them to marry, and a related superstition held that find-ing or unexpectedly being presented with a pair of gloves meant a wedding in the family before the year was out. Accidentally dropping your left glove was a sign that your lover was thinking of you, whereas a dropped right glove foretold the imminent arrival of a love letter. If your glove felt unusually tight when you put it on, it meant that you were loved.[3]

The supposed involvement of gloves in the progress of a love affair went further, for an elaborate 'language of gloves' allegedly allowed discreet communication between lovers. Delib-erately dropping both gloves meant 'I love you'; wearing the left glove half on, with thumb exposed, was a way of asking 'Do you love me?'; wearing the right glove in the same way was an invitation to be kissed; and smoothing one's gloves gently in the hand signified 'I wish I were here with you.' The signals could also fend off unwelcome attentions: striking one's chin with a glove was a way of saying 'I love another,' and lightly tossing a glove in the air meant 'I am engaged.'[4] These gestures seem so open to embarrassing misunderstandings that one wonders how often they were put into practice. Nevertheless the association between gloves and seduction was very real, and glove manu-facturers have often exploited it in their publicity material. A typical Van Raalte company advertisement from 1950s America shows a woman beckoning suggestively, her hand clad in sheer, pink, frilly nylon, as she demonstrates the brand's '"Come-hither" look in Nylon Sheerio gloves'.[5]

Pairs of gloves have played an important role in many court-ship rituals. In Estonia, where the tradition of knitting woollen mittens goes back more than eight hundred years, a young man's

Franz Hals, *Dorothea Berck*, 1644, oil on canvas. Dorothea wears a plain white glove on her right hand. In a companion portrait Hals shows her husband, Joseph Coymans, with a matching glove on his left hand, the paired gloves symbolizing the marriage bond.

"Come-Hither" look in Nylon Sheerio® gloves

How feminine can you be? *This* feminine—in Van Raalte's famous nylon
Sheerios—so light, so cool, so crisp, so daintily detailed—so pretty
to see your pink-tipped fingers through! And we don't have to tell you
how wonderfully they wash, dry in a flash and wear practically forever.
Nylon Sheerio gloves shown, $2.50 the pair at better stores everywhere.

—and Van Raalte is famous for
stockings and underthings, too

Van Raalte glove
advertisement,
1950. The
'"Come-hither"
look in Nylon
Sheerio gloves'
caption was
typical in
representing
gloves as
accessories
to seduction.

mother would send a bottle of spirits to the family of the girl he
wished to marry, and if the empty bottle came back with a pair
of knitted mittens attached to its neck, it meant that the suitor
was accepted.[6] In England, gloves were once associated with
stolen kisses: tradition had it that if a woman managed to kiss
a sleeping man without waking him, he was honour bound to
give her a pair of new gloves.[7] (Elizabeth Gaskell reverses the
roles in her novels *Mary Barton*, 1848, and *Sylvia's Lovers*, 1863,

where a sleeping woman is kissed by a man and owes him gloves
as a result.)

Flirtatious associations recur in the old Valentine's Day
custom that allowed girls to approach young men and ask to
be given new gloves at Easter. Some Valentine rhymes, such as
the one below, suggest that the glove-giving was a further stage
in a courtship that had already begun:

> The rose is red, the violet's blue,
> The gilly-flower sweet, and so are you;
> These are the words you bade me say
> For a pair of new gloves on Easter-day.[8]

Sometimes, however, gloves instigated a relationship. One
old English broadside ballad tells the story of a nobleman's
daughter who is due to marry a wealthy squire but who decides,
in defiance of social expectation, that she prefers the handsome
young farmer who has been appointed to give her away. Seeking
out the farmer in his fields, she deploys one of her richly decorated gloves to win his hand:

> She gave him a glove that was flower'd with gold,
> And told him she found it when coming along,
> As she was hunting with her dog and her gun.
> The young lady went home with a heart full
>   of love,
> And gave out a notice that she'd lost a glove;
> And the man that found it and brought it
>   to me,
> The man that did bring it her husband should be.
> The farmer was pleased when he heard of the
>   news,
> With a heart full of love to the lady he goes;
> Dear honoured lady I have picked up a glove,

And hope that you will be pleased to grant me your
    love.[9]

Which, of course, she does.

Popular rhymes such as these, involving lovers brought
together by a pair of gloves, are the everyday equivalents of fan-
tastic tales of gloves that perform the same function by magic,
and all confirm the association between glove and love. It is
unsurprising, then, that glove shops in fiction are often flirtatious spaces (as Samuel Pepys appreciated), where intimate
gestures of fitting and touching encourage familiarity between
the sexes.[10]

Despite the traditional association between paired gloves
and paired lovers, unpaired gloves too could display amorous
intent. John Reynolds imagines an unusually dramatic use of
gloves to signal ardour in his early seventeenth-century poem
Dolarnys Primrose, in which he describes lamenting women
'with woe-swollen eyes' watching from the shore as Julius
Agricola's fleet sets sail. In their grief, the women cast their
gloves into the sea, willing the waves to carry their love tokens
to the departing men.[11] Less ostentatiously, a single glove, still
warm from its wearer's hand, was commonly offered as a sentimental keepsake. It is said that after the death of George IV
more than a thousand mismatched ladies' gloves were found
among his possessions, preserved as intimate mementoes along
with love letters and locks of hair.[12]

By the nineteenth century, a woman's deliberately dropped
glove was a well-established flirtatious overture, recognized as an
open invitation to a man to restore it to its owner and engage in
conversation with her. It is the subject of Carolus-Duran's life-
size painting *The Lady with the Glove*, which had great success
when it went on show to the Paris public in 1869. Intentionally
dropped gloves often appear in novels, where they were a convenient device for bringing two characters together. Indeed,

the trope was used so frequently that some writers invented variations on the theme, introducing unexpected twists such as having the wrong person retrieve the glove, or treating the seductive gesture with ironic amusement, as in one nineteenth-century French novel where a naive young man is described as falling in love with

> the first young woman . . . to drop a little white
> glove that [he] could pick up, giving him both the
> opportunity and the courage to address a few words to
> her about the whiteness of a rather large hand which
> the little white glove enclosed with some difficulty.[13]

Gloves' amorous significance was not limited to flirtation and courtship, however. By the sixteenth century the custom of presenting them to wedding guests was widespread: a hundred pairs were distributed when the daughter of Henry Machyn, an English merchant, was married in 1560. Careful thought seems to have gone into the choice of wedding gloves, for in 1611 a bridegroom's anxious mother wrote of her difficulty in finding enough suitably impressive pairs to distribute, and had to change her plan when her preferred style was unavailable:

> I could not get so many Jessamy gloves as [I] wrote
> for; and at the last was fained to pick upon cordinant
> [gloves made of Cordova leather] for men and
> perfumed kid for women, I had them perfumed
> better than ordinary.[14]

It was not only at weddings of the wealthy that glove distribution was felt to be an essential part of the ceremonial. The practice was widespread; in a Robert Herrick poem of 1648 we see young country girls already planning 'What Gloves we'll give, and Ribbonings' as they fantasize about their future weddings.[15]

Although gloves handed out at marriage ceremonies would have helped to strengthen social bonds as much as those distributed at funerals did, wedding gloves had additional significance. An account of the marriage of a surgeon-apothecary and his bride in Wrexham in Wales in 1785 points to another meaning, for the gloves distributed there were not real. Instead, the whole neighbourhood was hung with glove-shaped paper decorations. As an eye-witness recalled:

> I saw at the Doors of his own and neighbours' Houses, throughout the street where he lived, large Boughs and Posts of Trees, that had been cut down and fixed there, filled with white paper, cut in the shape of Women's gloves, and of white Ribbons.[16]

Fluttering in the air, distributed across the neighbourhood but not presented to guests, these 'gloves' were purely decorative. Their shape and presence, however, was a reminder of gloves' old association with the binding marriage contract – a fitting way to mark the union of the new couple.

The custom of distributing gloves at weddings lasted well into the nineteenth century, but gloves' connection with the marriage ceremony could take other forms. Charles Dickens recorded a wedding ritual from the Low Countries – a ritual he described as 'odd' – in which gloves were as important as the wedding ring:

> The priest asks the bridegroom for a ring and a pair of gloves; red gloves, if they can be had; with three bits of silver money inside them. Putting the gloves into the bridegroom's right hand, he joins this with the right hand of the bride, and then, dexterously loosing them, he leaves the glove in the bride's grasp.[17]

Here the transfer of silver-filled gloves from husband to wife serves as a tangible symbol of the marriage contract, just as a soil-filled glove once confirmed the transfer of land ownership. Dickens disapproved of its implications, seeing it as 'a symbol, doubtless that [the bride] is taken possession of, bought and paid for and conquered like any other vassal'.[18] A less controversial wedding tradition involving a filled glove comes from Greece, where brides used to hide a lump of sugar inside their gloves to ensure that married life would be sweet.

Glove-related marriage customs cross many cultures, but they had particular force in the Netherlands. There, a betrothal was formally marked by the groom presenting his future bride with a pair of gloves, which were put on display before the marriage ceremony as a public emblem of the union about to be

Nicolaes Pickenoy, *Portrait of a Young Woman* (detail), 1632, oil on panel. The woman prominently displays a pair of ornate gloves in this portrait, painted to mark her marriage.

formalized.[19] Often highly ornate, like the richly embroidered and beribboned gloves trimmed with gold sequins depicted in Nicolaes Pickenoy's *Portrait of a Young Woman* of 1632, such gloves are a prominent feature of seventeenth-century Dutch marriage portraits, where their opulence – made more striking by being shown off against the traditional plain black silk of patrician wedding gowns – also signalled the new couple's wealth and status. But the power of the glove's symbolic value in marriage is demonstrated even more strikingly in the Netherlands by an old legal custom known as 'marriage with the glove', a form of marriage by proxy, where an empty glove stood for the vows of the absent bridegroom. A newspaper report from 1919 describes one such 'glove marriage' between a woman in Amsterdam and a man in Pretoria, South Africa:

> The bridegroom sent to his friend or best man in
> Amsterdam a power of attorney to represent him
> as his proxy at the ceremony, and at the same time
> forwarded his glove, which at the proper moment,
> when the two were made one, was held by both the
> bride and the proxy. The wedding was duly registered
> at Amsterdam and at Pretoria.[20]

Such marriages *met de handschoen* were not uncommon in the aftermath of the Second World War, when many single men emigrated to find work before sending home for a wife to join them. If one partner died before the couple could meet, the survivor still inherited the deceased's property in accordance with the law: the glove's role in the marriage ceremony made the union fully binding.

An old Danish folktale demonstrates just how deeply that association between gloves and the marriage pledge was embedded in popular culture. It is the story of a young king who is due to marry. When the time comes, his unattractive bride-designate

Swedish bridegroom's gloves, embroidered with hearts and flowers and decorated with sequins.

persuades a beautiful young kitchenmaid to take her place at the marriage ceremony, at which she is to receive a glove of special significance: 'It was the custom that the bride was given a glove in church; she held it in her hand when she took her marriage vows and would give it to her husband before they went to bed.' After the ceremony, the new 'queen' asks the maid to hand over the glove, but the maid refuses, saying that to do so would be to break the pledge made in church: 'I can't give it to you . . . I held it in my hand when I spoke the wedding vows. I must give it him myself.' The two women eventually agree that as the 'queen' enters the king's bedchamber on the royal wedding night, the maid will hide behind her and pass the glove to the king without being seen. When the hidden girl proffers the glove, however, the king – who had suspected the substitution all along – seizes her hand and pulls her to him, saying, 'You shall share my bed

. . . I am married to the girl who stood at my side in church and will have no other wife.'[21] Here the glove not only functions as a powerful emblem of the marriage vow, but ensures the union of a couple destined to be together, for in the end (as so often happens in fairy tales) the kitchenmaid is revealed to be a princess, the king's rightful bride.

It is not only in heterosexual relationships that gloves have special meaning, as can be seen from a sonnet by Richard Barnfield, a contemporary of Shakespeare, which is addressed to a young male lover:

> Here: hold this glove (this milk-white cheveril glove)
> Not quaintly over-wrought with curious knots,
> Not deckt with golden spangs, nor silver spots,
> Yet wholesome for thy hand as thou shall prove.
> Ah no; (sweet boy) place this glove neere thy heart,

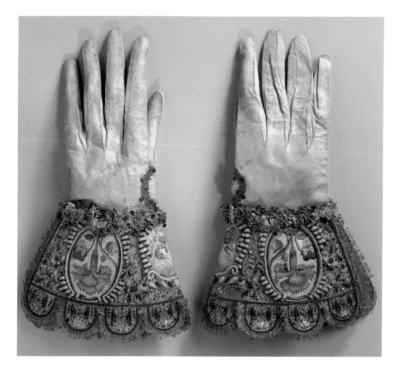

Bride's gloves, embroidered with carnations, wild strawberries and wood violets, symbols relating to love, fertility and fidelity. Netherlands, 1637.

Weare it, and lodge it still within thy brest,
So shalt thou make me (most unhappy), blest.[22]

Significantly, the poet does not offer his lover an ornately embroidered and spangled glove of the kind fashionable in the early seventeenth century when the poem was written, but one of plain white kid ('cheveril'): this glove represents not wealth and status but pure love. But like the glove exchanged in the bedchamber in the Danish tale, it also suggests carnal love, for a glove is like a second skin, following the contours of the hand, moving with it, and sometimes indistinguishable from it. The image of a glove being placed over the youth's heart evokes the poet's hand caressing the chest of the 'sweet boy'. Responding to the youth's imagined retort that 'A glove is for the hand not for the heart,' the poet ends the sonnet with a play on words that makes it clear that the glove's hand-covering function is less important than its symbolic value as a metaphor for love in all its senses:

If thou from glove do'st take away the g,
Then glove is love: and so I send it thee.[23]

Barnfield's teasing interplay between glove and hand may have been a literary device, but it was one that knowingly played on the erotic boundary between the two.

At times, that erotic potential has been deemed dangerously provocative, and fear of an indecent glimpse of a woman's ungloved hand has led to women being compelled to cover their hands at all times, as happens now in areas controlled by the Islamic State. The sixteenth-century Spanish humanist Juan Luis Vives likewise wanted women always to wear gloves, convinced that the sight of an uncovered female hand would inflame men's passions. The sole purpose of gloves was to preserve the hand's modesty, he insisted:

the more wanton, seeing a part of the body not usually
exposed to view, are enflamed as if they had caught
fire. For what purpose were long sleeves and gloves
invented? Was it to keep the hands snug in soft and
fragrant wrappings? Antiquity was not so ingenious
in luxury and self-indulgence. Certainly they were
invented out of necessity and so that except when
engaged in doing something, the hands would be
hidden and that no part of the body, vile and useless
servant, would be seen.[24]

Many of his contemporaries disagreed with this puritanical
attitude, however, and saw nothing wrong in the pleasurable
sight of a glove being removed to reveal a pretty hand. Indeed, in
The Book of the Courtier (1528) Baldassare Castiglione celebrated that effect, and argued that the drawing back on of a
glove only intensifies the desire to see the hand it conceals:

if they [the hands] are delicate and beautiful, and
occasionally left bare when there is no need to use
them, and not in order to display their beauty, they
leave a very great desire to see more of them, and
especially if covered with gloves again.[25]

Pulling a glove on or off allowed a glimpse of female flesh,
especially thrilling during periods when the hand was the only
part of the body, other than the face, occasionally to be seen
uncovered in public. Elizabeth i understood this when she
slowly removed one of her gloves to allow the French ambassador to admire her long, slim, pale fingers, and a suitor's gradual
or partial removal of a woman's glove is vital to descriptions of
sensual encounters in many nineteenth- and early twentieth-
century novels.[26] In Thomas Hardy's *The Woodlanders* (1887),
for example, Melbury is left in no doubt about the relationship

between Mrs Charmond and Dr Fitzpiers when he witnesses the following scene:

> Mrs Charmond had come up with the doctor, who
> was standing immediately behind the carriage. She
> had turned to him; her arm being thrown carelessly
> over the back of the seat. They looked in each other's
> faces without uttering a word, an arch yet gloomy
> smile wreathing her lips. Fitzpiers clasped her hanging
> hand, and, while she still remained in the same listless
> attitude, looking volumes into his eyes, he stealthily
> unbuttoned her glove, and stripped her hand of it by
> rolling back the gauntlet over the fingers, so that it came
> off inside out. He then raised her hand to his mouth,
> she still reclining passively, watching him as she might
> have watched a fly upon her dress . . . She snatched away
> her hand, touched the pony with the whip, and left him
> standing there, holding the reversed glove.[27]

If novelists could convey erotic tension by depicting the gradual unveiling of a hand, striptease artists exploited such tension to the full. The burlesque entertainer Gypsy Rose Lee is said to have spun out the removal of a single glove into a slow, titillating performance that lasted for a quarter of an hour, and the scene in the 1946 film *Gilda* where Rita Hayworth seductively peels off a long, black glove is an iconic moment in film history.

With gloves generating such erotic reactions, one might expect them to be a focus of fetishism, but in *Psychopathia Sexualis*, Richard von Krafft-Ebing's classic 1886 study of sexual deviation, the author observes that, compared to shoe fetishism, glove fetishism is rare. He explains:

> The female hand is usually seen uncovered; the foot,
> covered. Thus the early associations which determine

Rita Hayworth slowly removes a glove in the famous glove striptease scene from Charles Vidor's 1946 film, *Gilda*.

the direction of the vita sexualis are naturally connected with the naked hand, but with the covered foot.[28]

'Glove Fetishism' nevertheless currently merits a Wikipedia entry that gives particular emphasis to the erotic pleasures of tight-fitting latex gloves, while John Cleland's *Memoirs of a Woman of Pleasure* – the eighteenth-century erotic novel more commonly known as *Fanny Hill* – features 'a grave, staid, solemn elderly gentleman' whose glove fetishism takes a different form. His peculiarity of taste, says Fanny,

was to present me at once with a dozen pairs of the
whitest kid gloves: these he would divert himself with
drawing on me, and then biting off their fingers'
ends; all which fooleries of a sickly appetite the old
gentleman paid more liberally for than most others
did for more essential favours.[29]

Even when gloves are treated more conventionally, they retain a
certain fetishistic value when used as a surrogate for a desired
woman's hand or naked body, or when a hand entering or leaving a glove is depicted as an erotic act.

Representing a woman's desirability by means of a glove
was a particularly popular device in Renaissance literature. The
fourteenth-century Italian poet Petrarch devoted three of his
Canzoniere to the glove of his beloved Laura, although the real
focus of desire was the pink-and-white hand briefly glimpsed
beneath it:

White, delicate and precious little glove,
that covered flawless ivory and fresh roses . . .
I wish I had a part of that fine veil![30]

But when Laura puts her glove on again – when, as the poet
writes, her 'single naked hand . . . reclothes itself, to my deep
sorrow' – it is the remembered glove rather than the hand that
conjures up an ecstatic vision, safely distanced, of his beloved:

My luck, along with Love, had blessed me so
With an embroidery of gold and silk,
I'd almost reached the limits of my joy
By saying to myself, 'Just think who wore this!'[31]

That erotically charged relation between glove and hand
is reversed in Théophile Gautier's *Une Larme du diable* (The

Devil's Tear), a drama from 1839 in which Satan, in an attempt
to seduce two young sisters, sends everything in their room into
a state of sexual arousal. Usually gloves are seen from the outside, but Gautier looks within and gives a voice to the covered
hand of one of the girls. Under Satan's influence, the hand begs

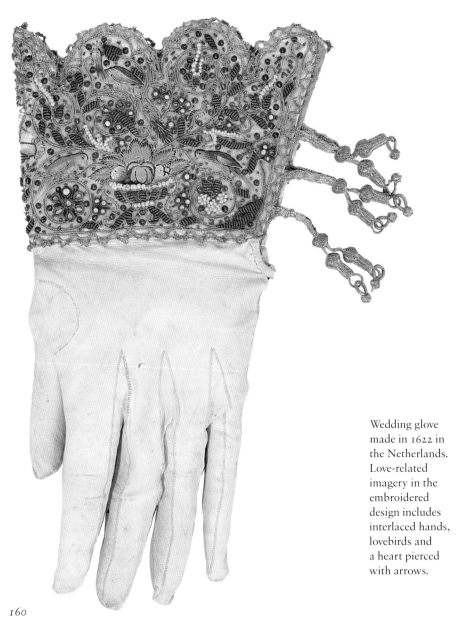

Wedding glove
made in 1622 in
the Netherlands.
Love-related
imagery in the
embroidered
design includes
interlaced hands,
lovebirds and
a heart pierced
with arrows.

its owner to free it from the constraints of its glove and let it be embraced by a lover instead:

> Shapely and beautiful as I am, all dimpled and with such slim fingers and such pink nails, do you really think . . . that I want to stay imprisoned inside a glove forever? For me, the best glove would be the hand of a young man, who would clasp me tenderly; the most beautiful ring would be a wedding ring.[32]

Often the distinction between hand and glove dissolves entirely, as a glove becomes an explicit metonym for a hand, and a hand, in turn, represents a woman's desired body. Woman and glove are conflated: yearning for a woman's body manifests itself as yearning for her glove. As Edmond de Goncourt writes of a character in his 1884 novel *Chérie*: 'The glove was the thing he most desired from a woman, it was the mould and imprint of her hand, an object that preserved some of the life of her fingers.'[33]

Offering or acquiring a glove as a love token acknowledged that identification between woman and glove: it was a gift whose tactility and intimate contact with naked flesh made it emotionally and erotically charged. Gustave Flaubert treasured a glove belonging to his mistress, Louise Colet, and kept it along with her love letters, telling her that its scent evoked the smell of her shoulder and the warmth of her bare arm.[34] And when the eccentric Madame du Titre was greeted by Friedrich Wilhelm III of Prussia, she was so delighted that he had touched her glove that she framed the 'precious relic' under glass with the risqué caption, 'The king squeezed me!'[35]

Whether worn publicly as a trophy or preserved and fetishized as a private memento of a love affair, women's gloves regularly appear in art and literature as emblems of passionate devotion, and are the recipients of ardent declarations of love. In his Elizabethan romance *The Old Arcadia*, Sir Philip Sidney describes Dorus's rapturous reaction to the glove of his beloved Pamela, and depicts him kissing and embracing it as if it were Pamela herself:

[Dorus] drew out a glove of Pamela's done with murrey silk and gold lace, and (not without tender tears kissing it) he put it again in his bosom, and sang these two stanzas:

> Sweet glove, the witness of my secret bliss
> . . . Be thou my star in this my darkest night
> . . . Be thou, sweet glove, the anchor of my mind,
> Till my frail bark his hav'n again do find.
> Sweet glove, the sweet despoils of sweetest hand,
> Fair hand, the fairest pledge of fairer heart (etc.)[36]

The fervent emotions aroused by glove mementos such as Pamela's could, however, attract ridicule. Just as the French ambassador in the *Heptameron* tale quietly mocks the English lord for worshiping the glove instead of winning the lady, the Victorian novelist Wilkie Collins pokes fun at a callow young man's reaction to a woman's glove in *No Name* (1862):

Noel Vanstone went home rapturously with a keepsake in his breast-pocket – he had taken tender possession of one of Miss Bygrave's gloves. At intervals during the day, whenever he was alone, he took out the glove, and kissed it with a devotion which was almost passionate in its fervour. The miserable little creature luxuriated in his moments of stolen happiness, with a speechless and stealthy delight which was a new sensation to him.[37]

If in instances such as these the glove serves as a veiled substitute for the woman's desired but absent body, in several

Renaissance texts it suggests an even closer union. Rather than admiring and fetishizing the beloved's glove, lovers dream of *becoming* that glove, to enjoy the closest physical intimacy. They want to press themselves against her skin like a glove, and hold her tight. In *Le Gan*, Godard claims that 'five hundred thousand lovers' would wish to be transformed into gloves in order to have the blissful intimacy of enclosing and fondling a lady's fingers.[38] It was a sentiment expressed in Barnabe Barnes's Sonnet LXIII:

> Would I were changed but to my Mistress' gloves,
> That those white lovely fingers I might hide!
> That I might kiss those hands, which mine heart loves![39]

and shared by Shakespeare's Romeo, who, on seeing Juliet leaning her cheek against her hand, sighs:

> O, that I were a glove upon that hand,
> That I might touch that cheek![40]

These literary fantasies of being transformed into a woman's glove pale, however, in comparison to the hyperbolic devotion expressed in a letter to Lady Penelope Rich from Antonio Pérez, an exiled Spaniard who arrived at the court of Elizabeth I in 1593. Lady Penelope had asked him for a pair of dogskin gloves, but the gloves that accompanied his letter were, he claimed, crafted not from any ordinary leather but from his own flayed skin:

> I have been so troubled not to have at hand the dog's
> skin gloves your Ladyship desires that, pending the
> time when they shall arrive, I have resolved to sacrifice
> myself to your service and flay a piece of my own skin
> from the most tender part of my body, if such an

uncouth carcass as mine can have any tender skin. To
this length can love and wish to serve a lady be carried
that a man should flay himself to make gloves for his
lady out of his own skin.[41]

With an extraordinarily graphic and excessive flourish, Pérez
has converted a conventional gift of gloves into an extravagant
conceit by which he offers himself to the lady. What 'the most
tender part of [his] body' was is left to the imagination.

Erotic meanings have long been attributed to gloves, and
it is easy to see how sexual connotations have evolved from
their warmth, softness and penetrability. The old French expression *perdre ses gants* (to lose one's gloves) referred to the loss
of a girl's virginity, and Gordon Williams's *Dictionary of Sexual
Language and Imagery in Shakespearean and Stuart Literature*
(1964) equates 'glove' with 'vagina' and lists many English examples, including a report of Prince Henry, son of James I, rejecting
the glove of a woman who had been unfaithful to him, on the
grounds that 'it is *stretcht* by another'.[42]

Although these examples relate gloves to female genitalia,
gloves' size and stiffness sometimes appear as a symbol of male
sexuality. In his discussion of medieval manuscript illustrations
of *The Romance of the Rose*, John V. Fleming notes that the
figure of the Lover is frequently depicted carrying a single, over-
sized glove 'quite obtrusively' and 'quite disconcertingly':

Whenever we see [the Lover] with it, it is a striking
reminder of his essential cupidity, the kind of love
which impels him. The glove is, so to speak, his proper
costume for the 'old dance'.[43]

In the nineteenth century, however, it was particularly
women's long, multi-buttoned gloves, as close-fitting as a second
skin, that were felt to have erotic connotations. The French

writer Alphonse Karr included the gesture of removing a glove to take holy water in his playful list of 32 infidelities a faithful wife could commit between home and church.[44] Novelists were quick to realize that an innocent glove could convey aspects of desire which propriety prevented them from describing directly, from the sensual delicacy of 'the little hand at work' as it buttons or unbuttons a glove, to the more shocking 'undressing' evoked by Guy de Maupassant in *Fort Comme la Mort* (Strong as Death; 1889) as he describes a long glove being peeled off to reveal the naked flesh beneath:

> She wore long gloves that came up to the elbow. To remove one, she took hold of it by the upper edge and slid it down rapidly, turning it inside out as if she were skinning a snake. The arm appeared, pale, plump and rounded, unclothed so quickly that it suggested the idea of complete, bold nudity.[45]

So explicit were the sexual overtones of a glove that appears in an early draft of *Madame Bovary* that Flaubert removed the passage before the novel was published in 1856. The deleted episode describes how Léon creeps downstairs in the night to retrieve a pale yellow glove dropped by Emma and takes it back to bed with him. The glove still bears her scent and retains the form of her hand – the imprints of her fingernails, creases over the joints, and the curve of the leather where it stretched across the fleshy base of her thumb. Léon sniffs it, kisses it, inserts his fingers into it, and eventually falls asleep with his face resting on it. 'Make it understood that he masturbates with this glove,' Flaubert noted in the margin, before deciding that it would be wiser not to.[46]

It was not only novelists who wove gloves and their connotations into their work. Painters, too, appreciated gloves' capacity to embody powerful feelings. Symbolist artists (who sought 'to

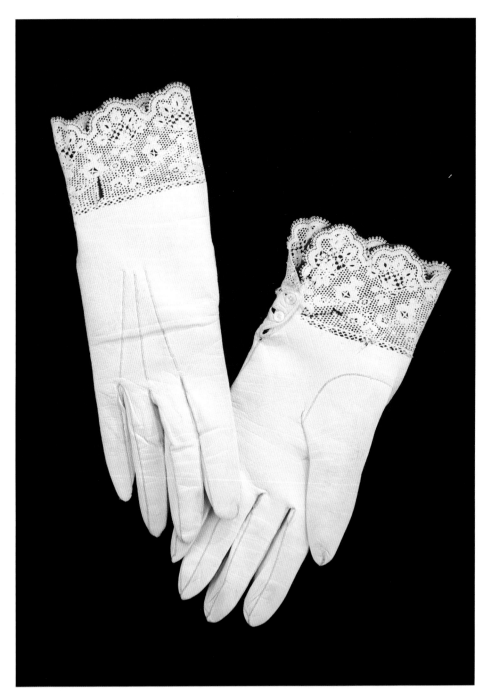

French wedding gloves of fine kid, delicately cut at the cuffs to resemble lace.
Préville, 1842.

depict not the thing but the effect it produces', as the French poet Stéphane Mallarmé put it) saw how usefully evocative gloves could be in their experiments to express psychological states by depicting familiar objects in unfamiliar contexts. A mysterious glove is at the centre of a series of ten etchings from 1877–8, entitled *Paraphrase on the Finding of a Glove*, by the German artist Max Klinger. The etchings show a glove dropped by a woman at an ice rink undergoing a sequence of dreamlike transformations; it is both the focus and expression of the artist's passionate but tormented desire. The enigmatic woman remains unseen, but from image to image tumultuous emotions – longing, despair, adulation, terror, sexual desire – are projected on to her eroticized glove as it fluctuates in size and dominance. The series ends with it lying suggestively agape, conquered at last by Cupid's dart.

Max Klinger, 'Amor (Cupid)', the final image in his narrative series of etchings *Paraphrase on the Finding of a Glove*, 1877–8.

    The identification of gloves with love or sexuality is not always so direct, however. Just as gloves can be turned inside out, so their symbolism can be reversed. Klinger's hallucinatory treatment of the glove in these etchings was greatly admired by the Italian artist Giorgio de Chirico, and in the years immediately before the First World War, strange, incongruous gloves,

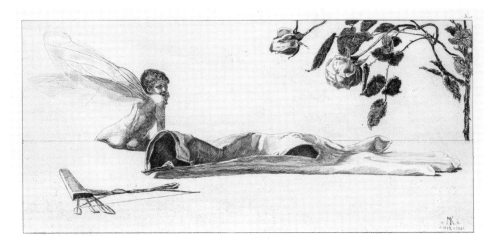

often of disproportionate size, start to appear in the latter's paintings. There they take on a changed meaning as he begins, in his words, 'to perceive the first ghosts of an art more complete, more profound, more complicated and . . . more metaphysical'. The source of this new artistic sensitivity he attributed to a large advertising sign in the form of a glove that hung outside a shop, which he depicted in his paintings *The Destiny of a Poet* and *Still-life: Turin, Spring* (both 1914). Inflexible, unwearable and strangely threatening, the huge glove for de Chirico indicated not joyous passion but its opposite – a disturbing, vacant sadness:

> New lands appeared on the horizon. The big zinc
> coloured glove, with the terrible golden nails, swung
> on the shop door in the sad breaths of the civic
> afternoons; with its index finger pointing toward
> the slabs of the sidewalk it showed me the hermetic
> signs of a new melancholy.[47]

With the help of a very different glove, that 'new melancholy' emerges from what is perhaps de Chirico's best known work, *The Song of Love*, also from 1914. It depicts an enormous, limp, red rubber glove, firmly nailed shut at the wrist and utterly devoid of gloves' traditional amorous associations, next to a plaster head of Apollo, a green ball and a locomotive. The disconcerting juxtaposition points to a fundamental dislocation that is deliberately at odds with the work's sentimental title.

It is hardly surprising that gloves' strange and flexible symbolism should have appealed to the Surrealists, who, like Flaubert, were intrigued by the disturbing quality of something that was so like and yet so unlike a hand. In the *Surrealist Manifesto* of 1924, André Breton enigmatically proclaimed that 'Surrealism . . . will glove your hand,' and in *Nadja* (1928) he described the extraordinary effect that a certain pair of sky-blue gloves had on him and his colleagues at the Surrealists' Paris headquarters.⁴⁸ The gloves were worn by fellow Surrealist Lise Deharme when she paid a visit, and the flippant suggestion that she should donate one of them to the group made Breton fear that she might indeed remove a glove and place it on the table. Later, Deharme returned to leave a heavy, bronze mould of a glove on the very spot on the table that her soft blue glove might have occupied. In recounting his alarm and his subsequent fascination with the metal glove, Breton draws attention to gloves' disquieting undertones.⁴⁹ Weighty, solid, inflexible, unpaired and of course unwearable, Deharme's bronze glove is the antithesis of everything that characterizes a glove. It was bestowed in a distorted variant of the glove as love token, and everything about it destabilizes the accepted concept of a glove and its conventional associations. It is a quintessentially Surrealist object, an uncanny emblem of modernity.

Pablo Picasso, the grandson of a glove-maker, found gloves equally intriguing, and they often feature in his early work. Three were of great and contrasting significance to him. Two were the dainty pair that his lover Dora Maar was wearing in 1936 when he saw her for the first time as she sat in the Café les Deux Magots in Paris, repeatedly stabbing a sharp penknife into the table between her gloved fingers. Sometimes she missed, and drops of blood appeared between the little roses embroidered on her gloves. Picasso asked to have them, and he preserved them along with other mementoes in a curious reversion to the romantic trope of glove as love token, but these blood-spotted gloves also memorialized pain.

The other glove, which he kept for many years, was utterly different in form and meaning, and carried horrific resonance. It was a large, leather glove for a man's right hand, and had come from Guernica, the Basque town to whose devastation by bombing in April 1937 Picasso had responded in his famous painting of the same name. Preliminary work for his *Guernica* includes drawings of the glove, and it reappears in the bottom left of the finished painting as the hand of the dead man. As he explained to a journalist in 1970: 'The man who wore it died in the destruction, his hands contorted in death. This is a tortured object found on the battlefield of liberty.' As a 'tortured object', the single, distorted glove embodied for Picasso the devastated town he had called 'the most tortured object in the world'. It did so in multiple ways, as art critic Brian Sewell has noted:

> That the glove itself was of singular importance to Picasso as relic, idea, image, tortured object and even work of art – as is suggested by his signature, scrawled in purple ink across the gauntlet – there can be no doubt; it explains, at last, Picasso's obstinate retention of a right hand for the fallen warrior when it should be left, for it is a right-hand glove. It may well be the only surviving memento of the 1,645 Guernicans killed and the 889 wounded.[50]

Works such as his *Composition with Glove* (1930) – a sand-covered construction made from a glove, cardboard and sewn and glued plant material – show Picasso seeking to dissolve the boundaries between art genres, and in gloves he may have recognized an ideal representation of flexible boundaries. The dissolving borderline between hand and glove was captured particularly memorably in a creation he produced in 1937 for Man Ray to photograph, when he applied paint directly to a woman's hands to make them look unsettlingly like gloves, one black, one white, with decorative cuffs and points, but also with painted fingernails.

Picasso was not alone in being fascinated by that uneasy relationship between body and glove, for around the time that he was making hands look like gloves, the Swiss-German Surrealist artist Meret Oppenheim was collaborating with fashion designer

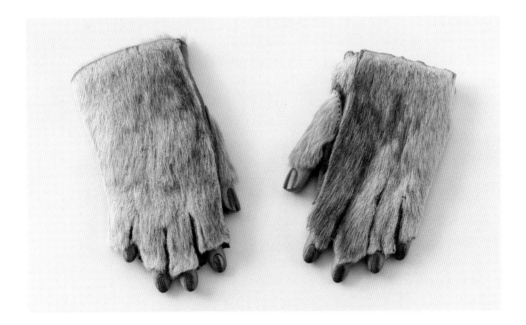

Meret
Oppenheim,
*Fur Gloves
with Wooden
Fingers*, 1936.
The strange
and flexible
symbolism
of gloves had
particular
appeal for
the Surrealists.

Elsa Schiaparelli to create gloves that looked like hands. With scarlet or gold fingernails, or resembling an X-ray of the hand's bone structure, these were gloves designed to draw attention to what they hid. So, too, were her startling gloves of animal fur from which wooden fingers with scarlet fingernails emerge in an incongruous fusion of animality and superficial glamour. Much later, in 1985, Oppenheim returned to the theme and produced grey goatskin gloves, screenprinted with the hand's network of red blood vessels, once again dissolving the boundary between hand and glove that so intrigued the Surrealists, and challenging the sentimentality of the glove/love association.

The Surrealists were not the first to disturb that association. If paired gloves were seen as emblematic of a love match or a marriage union, and if a single glove might lead to a partner and a pairing, single gloves could equally well represent the opposite: an absence of love. A lone glove, lost and useless without its partner, is usually discarded, and so, despite gloves' long history as love tokens and fetishized mementoes, a single glove may symbolize the unloved or abandoned. This is what happens in Francis Beaumont and John Fletcher's Renaissance drama *The Scornful Lady*, where a man refuses to acknowledge the usual seductive symbolism of a glove dropped by a woman in an attempt to attract him, and instead heaps derision on the glove as a cheap, smelly artefact with no hidden powers. The single glove is scorned as unpaired and useless, and in rejecting it, he contemptuously rejects the woman:

> Here's Dogskin and Storax sufficient to kill a Hawk
> . . . hark you Mistress, what hidden Virtue is there in
> this Glove, that you would have me wear it? Is't good
> against sore Eyes, or will it charm the Tooth-ach?
> Or these red tops, being steept in White-wine soluble,
> wil't kill the Itch? Or has it so conceal'd a Providence
> to keep my Hand from Bonds? If it have none of these,
> and prove no more but a bare Glove of half a Crown

The apparent pathos of a single, lost glove has inspired writers, artists and photographers.

a pair, 'twill be but half a courtesy, I wear two always,
faith let's draw cuts, one will do me no pleasure.[51]

Another unattractive glove, wrinkled and old, is given a more poignant interpretation in 'Glove', a twentieth-century poem by the Australian author Margaret Scott. While evoking its owner's once-stylist past, the lone, unwanted, 'widowed' glove encapsulates the fading of life and love:

> At the back of this old drawer there's a lost glove,
> crinkled, lifeless, dry as a sloughed skin –
> a kid glove with tiny raised seams
> that ran between the knuckles in the days
> when every lady matched her hats and bags
> and cocked her head before she went into town,
> judging a gloved hand held at arm's length
> like a mirror.
>
> But this is a poor black widow.
> Impossible to imagine any lover
> gathering it up to cherish as a favour,
> yearning over its freedom to touch a cheek,
> plotting to carry it back where it makes a pair.
> Loss has made it useless and absurd.[52]

Although the glove is a repository of memories, it has not been kept or cherished as a memento, and the images of seduction so often linked to gloves are 'impossible to imagine'. Once again, a glove proves its ability to flip itself inside out both physically and symbolically, here demonstrating that if gloves can evoke desire, courtship, marriage and sex, they can also convey love's very absence.

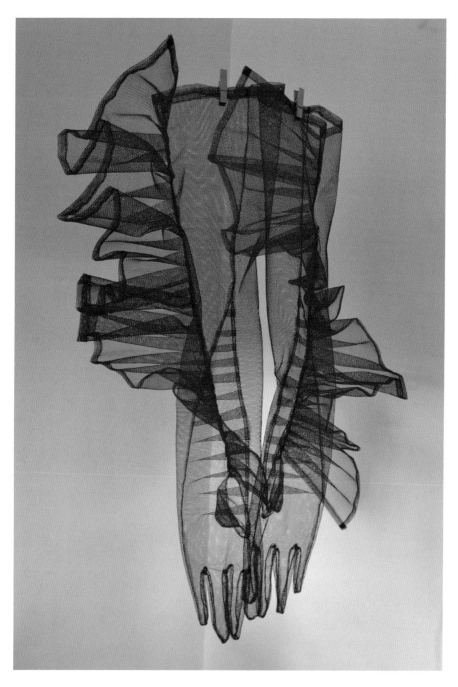

'Rays' gloves in deadstock tulle from Taylor-Bea Gordon's T-LABEL company.
Eye-catching, photogenic gloves such as these have gained much publicity
thanks to social media.

SIX

Archers, Artists and Astronauts: Functions Old and New

Whether seen as protecting hands, uniting lovers, guaranteeing contracts, honouring pledges, conveying messages, proclaiming status, confirming identity, sealing marriages, signalling probity or enacting magic, it is clear that gloves' roots in Western culture run deep. The list of positive qualities attributed to them is astonishingly long and varied. Yet so, too, are the accusations levelled against them. As we have seen, gloves have attracted disapproval and distrust since earliest times. Whether suspected of covering up the truth, inciting lust, concealing demonic powers, betraying moral or physical weakness or denoting a reviled social class, they have often been subject to condemnation. Even at the height of their nineteenth-century popularity there were glimmers of discontent. Perhaps it was inevitable that a once exclusive accessory that was increasingly being worn by all social classes should begin to lose its cachet, although it took a long time for gloves' desirability to wane.

In France, in the 1880s, Baroness Staffe had already observed that some gentlemen had become so exasperated by the lower classes' adoption of gloves that they went out in public barehanded as a way of marking their own distinction and superiority. Staffe strongly disapproved of this behaviour:

> It is a form of protest, a kind of opposition ever since the glove became democratised . . . men wishing to distinguish themselves tossed their gloves to the backs

of drawers and flaunted their fine hands, telling all
and sundry that it takes five centuries of leisure in
one's bloodline to acquire a beautiful hand. What
pretentious stupidity![1]

Bertall, too, had noticed that one of his aristocratic acquaintances with very elegant hands always kept hold of his gloves
instead of putting them on, claiming that only people with
deformed hands needed to wear them. 'I believe he is in the
wrong,' wrote Bertall, who, like Staffe, condemned such conduct.[2] But it was a sign that attitudes to glove-wearing were
again starting to change.

Like Gustave Flaubert, who had complained in the 1850s
that gloves stifled creativity, there were many who saw them as
symbols of social constraint. Novelists began to create characters who found glove-wearing uncomfortably restrictive, not
only physically but psychologically: to them, tight-fitting gloves
represented oppressive conformity. Dorothea Brooke, the hero-
ine of George Eliot's *Middlemarch* (1871–2), is seen 'throwing
off her bonnet and gloves, with an instinctive discarding of formality' and, later, taking off her gloves 'from an impulse which
she could never resist when she wanted a sense of freedom'.[3]

Despite the reluctance of some, however, gloves remained an
essential part of everyday dress, although by the early twentieth
century signs of resistance like that of Dorothea were beginning
to appear more frequently. In Frances Cornford's 1910 poem 'To
a Fat Lady Seen From a Train', the mere fact that the woman is
wearing gloves is enough to portray her as stuffy, unattractive
and somewhat ridiculous:

O why do you walk through the fields in gloves,
Missing so much and so much?
O fat white woman whom nobody loves,
Why do you walk through the fields in gloves,

When the grass is soft as the breast of doves
And shivering sweet to the touch?
O why do you walk through the fields in gloves,
Missing so much and so much?

Far from being seductive or indicating an enviable social status, the gloves of this 'fat white woman whom nobody loves' are seen as a barrier to sensuality that prevents her from engaging with her surroundings. Reversing gloves' conventional attributes, Cornford represents the gloved woman as unlovely, unloved and out of touch with the world around her. By choosing to wear gloves, she has deprived herself of sensual pleasure and of much else.

That attitudes to gloves were beginning to change is also hinted at by Virginia Woolf, in whose work gloves often help to articulate wider ideas about social change. Her 1922 short story 'Mrs Dalloway in Bond Street' opens with the words: 'Mrs Dalloway said she would buy the gloves herself,' and it ends with Mrs Dalloway purchasing the perfect pair: 'Half an inch above the elbow; pearl buttons; five and a quarter.' But woven through Woolf's account of that purchase is a sombre awareness of the recent war and the changes it has brought. 'Gloves have never been quite so reliable since the war,' observes the shop assistant when a new glove splits as a customer tries it on.[4] The simple act of buying a pair of gloves is transformed into a poignant reflection on change and loss and empty sacrifice. 'Thousands of young men had died that things might go on,' reflects Mrs Dalloway as the assistant finally brings her the desired French gloves that were fashionable before the war: the appalling disproportion between war dead and pretty gloves needed no further comment.

In Woolf's novel *Mrs Dalloway*, published three years later, the relative absence of gloves is significant. As in the short story, gloves (or their absence) become a touchstone for changing times

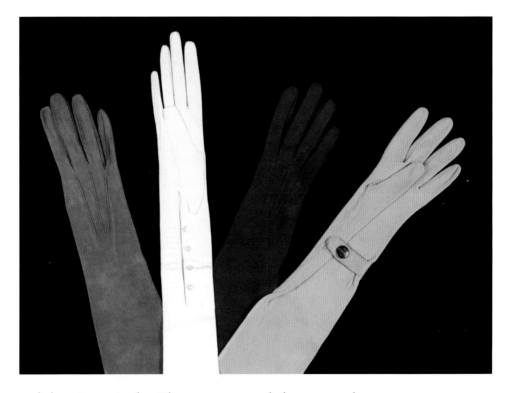

and changing attitudes. They now seem to belong to an almost bygone age. The novel's famous first sentence echoes the words of the short story's opening, but now it is flowers, not gloves, that Mrs Dalloway says she will buy herself. Walking up Bond Street and 'pausing for a moment at the window of a glove shop where, before the war, you could buy almost perfect gloves', she reflects that 'her old uncle William used to say a lady is known by her shoes and her gloves.'[5] Although Mrs Dalloway may agree with her old uncle about the importance of gloves, to a new generation they represent a social code that has become outdated and irrelevant: 'Gloves and shoes; she had a passion for gloves; but her own daughter, her Elizabeth, cared not a straw for either of them.'[6]

Glove-wearing continued nevertheless, surviving austerity restrictions during the Second World War, when buying a pair

Women's gloves in various lengths and colours. France, 1910s.

meant using up precious clothing-ration coupons. In Britain their manufacture was subject to wartime Utility regulations, so styles became simpler and fancy cuffs and trims disappeared. In ways very different from Virginia Woolf's vision, gloves were again caught up in the repercussions of a world war, and the hand-knitting of warm versions for the troops was promoted as a public duty. Schools and organizations such as the Women's Institute were sent knitting patterns and supplies of wool, and the great quantities of gloves they packed up for distribution to soldiers and prisoners of war reflected the knitters' sympathy and patriotism and their desire to contribute to the war effort. During this period women knitted gloves for themselves more than ever before, often reusing wool unravelled from old knit-wear to avoid rationing, and adding extra-long wristbands to keep themselves warm at a time of fuel shortages.

Some manufacturers in the United States implied that buying their gloves was a patriotic duty, as is suggested in this 1942 advertisement for Kayser gloves, with its subtle references to

Women's leather gloves from the 1940s. A CC41 logo inside certified that the simple style complied with wartime Utility regulations.

army, nation, duty, efficiency, co-operation and tough, practical resilience:

> HAND-IN-GLOVE WITH AMERICA'S NEW DUTIES . . .
> KAY-CREPE . . . rayon fabric for Americans with *no* time
> on their hands!
>
> Takes wear and tear like a buck private . . . washes
> in a split second . . . keeps its shape . . . emerges from
> suds fresh and new. Kayser designs it with the practical
> beauty you want in your clothes right now. 1.00 a pair.[7]

After the war, glove-wearing enjoyed a resurgence. In America, with the Great Depression at an end, wages at record levels and the economy booming, new glove styles reflected and celebrated the new prosperity, as *Life* magazine's vivid description of glove-related glamour and excess in 1946 makes clear:

> This winter, ladies' gloves are more glittery than they
> have been since the days of Queen Elizabeth. Four
> centuries ago ladies' gloves sparkled with diamonds,
> rubies, pearls, emeralds and gold. This year ladies'
> dress gloves are made of bright fabrics and cobwebby
> lace, ornamented with sequins, jet, gilt thread and
> many jewels. The jewels, unlike Elizabeth's, are fake.
>
> The return of the glitter glove is part of the
> general urge to dress up in showy, extravagant clothes.
> The gloves shown on these pages cost from $5 to about
> $25 a pair. A short while after getting them, probably
> half the wearers will have lost one or both of their
> lovely new gloves. For no accountable reason, women
> lose more gloves than earrings, bracelets, pocketbooks
> or any other dress accessory. Unless they mend their
> ways, they will in 1946 drop and fail to retrieve more
> than a million gloves.[8]

'Hand-knit Essentials for the Forces'. Jaeger's wartime knitting patterns included woollen gloves for the military. England, mid-1940s.

These dropped gloves no longer signalled attempts at seduction; they were a symptom of carefree luxury and extravagance, the antithesis of wartime constraint.

With austerity restrictions no longer in force, even designers of less flamboyant gloves were free to experiment with new styles to suit the new mood of optimism. Gloves were produced for every occasion in different lengths, cuts and colours, many ornamented with buttons, bows, embroidery or ruffles. They came in new artificial fabrics, too, which were promoted as irresistibly delicate yet convenient and durable and fashionably modern, as in a 1951 American advertisement for Van Raalte gloves:

> *Tailored or Feminine – Van Raalte gloves you in* NYLON
> From early spring till late summer, from morning till
> night – whatever your costume – you'll wear nylon
> gloves by Van Raalte . . . Choose *Nylon Reindoe*, like
> creamiest doeskin, or *Nylon Sheerio*, like dreamiest
> cobwebs, all, *all nylon* – with the delicate air, the
> wonderful wear, the washability that puts all other
> gloves to shame. In good colors, at better stores,
> everywhere.[9]

Enthusiasm for wearing gloves 'from morning till night' was waning, however, and by the mid-1960s the disregard shown by Mrs Dalloway's daughter was widely shared. At a time of loosening social manners and dissolving class structures, the formality of regular glove-wearing seemed increasingly anachronistic.

Although they are no longer an essential part of everyday wear, except, perhaps, in the coldest of weather, gloves nevertheless continue to multiply and diversify in both form and function. The vast majority of gloves sold today are designed not for fashion or comfort, but to fulfil a specific requirement.

Disposable rubber gloves, the most obvious example, are needed around the world, and were being produced in the hundreds of billions each year before the COVID-19 pandemic forced an even greater surge in output. Thin and flexible, moulding themselves perfectly to the hand, medical gloves' main function is to form a protective barrier to prevent the transfer of infection. More subtly, they also create a psychological barrier between patient and practitioner, signalling the professional nature of the intimate contact about to take place. In that context they have been described as 'props in a theatre aimed at de-sexualizing nakedness', where they send a message quite contrary to the flirtatious signals gloves sometimes transmit.[10] Although many millions of them end up in landfill each year, some disposable gloves undergo a magical transformation when recycled into raw material for park benches, waste bins or watering cans.[11]

It is not only medical gloves that have seen a huge increase in recent years. Never have sports gloves been so diverse or so specialized, although gloves to suit various types of sport have been made for centuries. As the Hellenistic sculpture of the *Boxer at Rest* shows so clearly, gloves have been designed to protect and strengthen the hand in sport or combat since ancient times. Medieval hawking gloves were constructed to cushion the hand against the sharp talons that would land on it. Special gloves were made for early players of real tennis in the days before the introduction of racquets, when the ball was struck with the hand. (A Scottish ballad commemorating the murdered 'Bonnie Earl O' Moray' indicates his prowess at the game with the line, 'he played at the glove.')

Equestrians, too, needed appropriate gloves, although the type decreed by Antoine de Pluvinel, Louis XIII's riding master, was designed as much for display as for practicality. 'Appropriateness and comfort of dress' were essential on horseback, said Pluvinel, stipulating that

the gloves should be long and wide on the arm about
four good inches high to protect one from the sun,
and should be embroidered or garnished with gold
or silver, or, at least, there should be a fringe of silk
along the border of the same colour as the dress or the
colour of the ribbon of the hat or the belt, which must
also be similar.[12]

A similar focus on both aesthetics and sporting function
is evident in the nineteenth-century Japanese archer's gloves
shown here. While their chamois leather is beautifully decorated with circular designs and lined in finely patterned green
silk, they are also designed for practicality, with reinforced fingers and long straps to keep them securely in place during use.

Pair of Japanese
archer's gloves
in patterned
chamois leather
with a patterned
green silk lining,
19th century.

Nowadays the demand for gloves specifically designed to enhance performance in an innumerable variety of sports is vast. Baseball gloves – 'the most American glove of all', according to *American Pastoral*'s Levov – are bought in their millions, with around 4.5 million sold annually in the u.s. Such is their iconic status that in 2014 the French company Hermès created an exquisitely hand-stitched baseball glove in 'gold swift calfskin', whose ostentatious price tag of $14,100 drew much publicity for the luxury brand.

For many years, however, baseball was played barehanded. Gloves' first use in the game dates from about 1870, and in the early days players sometimes placed a piece of steak inside their glove as improvised protective padding, although many considered that wearing a glove to play was unmanly and un-sportsmanlike. Charlie Waitt, one of the first professional players to wear baseball gloves, was taunted for doing so, and adopted flesh-coloured mitts in the hope that they would be less notice-able to spectators. That attitude to gloves persists in other sports, as British footballer Gary Lineker has pointed out: 'Even these days, when the use of additional layers gets a far easier ride, you will still hear people moaning about footballers who wear gloves, and accusing them of lacking bottle.'[13] After Bill Doak, a star baseball player, suggested to a glove manufacturer that a glove's thumb and forefinger could be connected with webbing to create a natural ball trap, baseball glove design changed dramatically, and in turn changed the game itself, for the 'Bill Doak' glove, patented in 1922, was as much a sports device as a protective hand covering.

Manufacturers now use 3D and 4D technology to design baseball gloves, with variants for every playing position. A few produce custom-made gloves, using a mould of the player's hand to achieve the perfect fit, but to ensure fair play profession-als' gloves must conform to detailed specifications issued by the governing body of Major League Baseball. For example:

The catcher may wear a leather mitt not more than thirty-eight inches in circumference, nor more than fifteen and one-half inches from top to bottom. Such limits shall include all lacing and any leather band or facing attached to the outer edge of the mitt. The space between the thumb section and the finger section of the mitt shall not exceed six inches at the top of the mitt and four inches at the base of the thumb crotch. The web shall measure not more than seven inches across the top or more than six inches from its top to the base of the thumb crotch. The web may be either a lacing, lacing through leather tunnels, or a center piece of leather which may be an extension of the palm, connected to the mitt with lacing and constructed so that it will not exceed any of the above mentioned measurements.[14]

Baseball mitts are now of a size and shape that could not possibly be mistaken for a human hand, but despite their strange form, technical construction and stringent specifications, they seem capable of inspiring emotions normally reserved for intimate relationships. Once again, gloves intertwine with love, and Torii Hunter, nine times winner of the annual Gold Glove award for outstanding baseball players, uses a telling analogy to explain the powerful emotions involved in finding the right glove:

It's like a relationship, you just know. You start dating a girl, you hang out with her a couple of times, you know this is the one for you. After a year, you get comfortable and you figure out whether she's the real deal.

One glove designer talks of baseball players' unswerving loyalty to their chosen gloves, and points out that most remain faithful to the same model for their entire career: 'there's just something about it. They just can't bring themselves to try something different.' So personal is the relationship with the chosen gloves that many professional players give them names – usually female names. Coco, Sheila, Susan and Delicious have all accompanied Hunter on the baseball field.[15]

Most sports have their own specialist gloves. Archers, cricketers, fencers, golfers, ice-hockey players, motorcyclists, pole dancers, surfers, skydivers and more can choose from a range of gloves specially created to suit each purpose. Designs evolve as new refinements are added and new materials introduced, adapting to changes in the sport itself.

Driving gloves are a good example. When Dorothy Levitt, the first British female racing driver and a pioneer of women's motoring, published *The Woman and the Car: A Chatty Little Handbook for All Women Who Motor or Who Want to Motor* in 1909, she included advice on what women should wear on their hands when driving:

> Regarding gloves – never wear woollen gloves, as wool slips on the smooth surface of the steering-wheel and prevents one getting a firm grip. Gloves made of good, soft kid, fur-lined, without a fastening, and made with just a thumb, are the ideal gloves for winter driving . . . [T]he majority of work on a car (filling tanks, &c. &c.) can be done just as well if one's hands are protected by a pair of wash-leather gloves. You will find room for these gloves in the little drawer under the seat of the car.

That drawer, 'the secret of the dainty motoriste', was the forerunner of what is still called a glove compartment, though glove compartments in today's cars rarely contain gloves. Only the name is left as a reminder of its original purpose, which, according to Levitt, was to provide space not only for 'a pair of clean gloves, [but] an extra handkerchief, clean veil, powder-puff (unless you despise them), hair-pins and ordinary pins, a hand-mirror – and some chocolates are very soothing, sometimes!'[16] One photograph in her book shows Levitt sitting in an open car with the drawer pulled out to reveal a slim pair of pale chamois gloves, and others show her driving or attending to her vehicle in elegant, close-fitting gloves that look no different from everyday ladieswear.

Soon it was realized that a better adapted glove could make driving in an unheated open car with rudimentary suspension a less uncomfortable experience, and until the 1930s the standard motorist's glove was a thick leather gauntlet, drawn up over the sleeve to shut out chill winds, and lined with wool or fur for warmth and to help absorb vibrations. As car design improved, driving gloves evolved accordingly. Heated, enclosed cars with better shock absorbers and smoother suspension meant that heavy gauntlets were no longer appropriate. More important was for the driver to have a secure grip on the wheel and to be able to feel and control the vehicle's behaviour, and so gauntlets gave way to thin leather gloves, short and close-fitting, which allowed for more sensitivity and had string backs or perforated vent holes to prevent the hands from perspiring and losing grip on the wheel. Later, the introduction of non-slip steering wheels and power steering meant that driving gloves were no longer needed except by racing drivers, who require heat- and flame-proof gloves in high-visibility colours; the most advanced now incorporate a

Early woman motorist wearing long leather gauntlets. Driving gloves evolved in step with car design in the 20th century.

chip sensor in the palm area to monitor the driver's blood pressure and heart rate.

In Japan, people who drive for a living – taxi drivers, bus drivers, train drivers – commonly wear gloves of white cotton. Originally adopted to make the driver's hand signals more visible, today they have little practical function and are worn more for the subliminal messages they project. 'I feel more professional when I'm wearing white gloves. It looks smarter too,' reported one taxi driver, and a bus driver said he wore them to look 'clean' and 'trustworthy' – no doubt the reason why Japanese politicians often wear white gloves on the campaign trail.[17]

Although fine leather driving gloves with their distinctive perforations and short cut-away design are no longer necessary for normal driving, they have evolved again to become something of a fashion statement. When asked to pick a favourite piece from her company's luxury collection, Gizelle Renee, British Glover of the Year in 2017, chose a pair of scarlet leather driving gloves. 'My oh my do heads turn in those sexy little numbers!', she explained.[18] Appreciated for style rather than function, helped by appearing in films on glamorous hands such as those of 'The Driver' (Ryan Gosling) in *Drive* (2011) or James Bond (Daniel Craig) in *Spectre* (2015), driving gloves are now marketed as emblems of the wearer's discrimination and panache. The sports and racing car manufacturer Ferrari advertises luxurious driving gloves 'in soft lambskin nappa leather [which] feature the classic vents on the back of the hand and knuckles and boast impeccable taste'. Suggestive of a lifestyle both discerning and dynamic, they are described as 'Elegant and feisty like a single-seater dashing round the track', as if, like Ferrari's woollen pair whose non-slip palms are said to echo 'the power of the tyres speeding across the asphalt', the gloves have absorbed the speed and daring of the sport itself and will transfer something of its excitement to the wearer. Encouraging that daydream, the company offers 'fun' gloves for teenagers in designs and colours inspired by the racing gloves of professional Ferrari drivers; they are 'dedicated to young fans who yearn for the adrenaline of the racetrack'.[19]

Such gloves are more about fantasy and display than function, but many recent developments in glove design focus on a range of practical needs. Gloves created from new materials have been specifically devised to protect the hands from hazardous chemicals, or from high voltage, or flames, or powerful vibrations or extremes of temperature. Gloves made from cut-resistant material provide protection from blades or sharp instruments, and versions with specially textured palms and fingers allow the safe handling of slippery, wet or oily goods. Close-fitting compression gloves in thermal materials promise pain relief to arthritis sufferers.

Further diversification has extended the hand's capabilities in ingenious ways, although some innovations may be as short-lived as the gloves proposed by Louisa Llewellin, an Englishwoman who in 1904 registered a patent for 'Gloves for Self-defence and Other Purposes'. Tipped with sharp steel claws, Llewellin's gloves were designed to be worn on railway journeys, and were intended 'more especially for the use of ladies who travel alone and are therefore liable to be assailed by thieves and others'. As their inventor explained:

> The object is to provide means whereby a person's
> face can be effectually disfigured and the display
> of the article which forms the subject of my
> invention would speedily warn an assailant of
> what he might expect should he not desist from
> pursuing his evil designs, and the fact that he
> would in the case of persistence be sure to receive
> marks which would make him a noticeable figure
> would act as a deterrent . . . and be so severely

A butcher's safety glove in stainless steel chain mail.

scratched as to effectually prevent the majority of people from continuing their molestations.[20]

There is no evidence that Llewellin's gloves were ever made.

Barely more successful was the lethal Sedgley oss gun-glove, designed for use by the u.s. Office of Naval Intelligence during the Second World War. This was a single cowhide glove, intended to be worn half-concealed by the sleeve of a uniform. Attached to the back was a tiny, single-shot .38 Smith & Wesson pistol with a plunger that would fire a shot point-blank into the victim if the wearer punched him with a closed fist. Although around two hundred of these were manufactured, there is no record of the gun-glove having been fired.

Imaginative new ideas continue to appear for gloves that help the hand, however. There are gardening gloves with a claw at the end of each finger for digging and raking the soil without tools; pet-grooming gloves to remove dirt and loose hair from cats or dogs while stroking them; dishwashing gloves with silicone bristles on the palms to aid plate-scrubbing; and web-fingered swimming gloves to help wearers propel themselves through the water more swiftly and efficiently.

Glove design constantly changes to keep pace with a changing world. Not only do many gloves now have conductive threads woven into their fingertips to let them work on touch-screens but there are also Bluetooth-enabled gloves incorporating tiny speakers, microphones, circuit boards and batteries, which effectively transform the hand into a mobile phone. 'Talking gloves' for the deaf community have come a long way since George Dalgarno's seventeenth-century version, and some now vibrate to spell out an incoming text message on the wearer's hand.

Other gloves have inbuilt LED lights that effectively turn the hand into a torch. Some can flash or glow or change colour, for wear in nightclubs or at festivals, where they have given rise to the phenomenon of 'gloving' – a dance form that generates a light show from the rhythmical movements of hands clad in gloves with luminous or flashing fingers. A more practical deve-lopment is the smart motorbike glove, a gauntlet with bright LED lights on the back that flash to show when the rider is about

The Sedgley OSS.38 'gun glove' designed for use by the U.S. Navy during the Second World War.

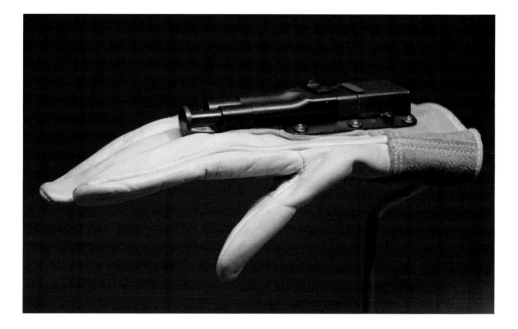

Gardening gloves
with claws for
raking, digging
and weeding.

to change direction, and can be operated automatically by the bike's indicators. Motorcyclists, like skiers, also have the option of electrically heated gloves to keep hands warm in the coldest conditions.

For gamers, special gloves claiming to 'eliminate fatigue and enhance blood flow' allow play to continue for longer periods, while for virtual reality enthusiasts there are gloves incorporating 'advanced vibrotactile actuators', with haptic feedback to immerse the wearer in a world of simulated experience. Electronic gloves, advertised as 'the world's most advanced wearable musical instrument', enable musicians to compose and perform music by gesturing with their hands.[21] Special gloves have even been developed to be worn not by humans but by robots. These rubber gloves with inbuilt sensors allow robotic hands to acquire a human sense of touch so sensitive that their fingers can delicately pick up a raspberry without crushing it.

Many of these developments have their origins in space technology, for space travel presents special challenges for glove design. In outer space, as NASA explains:

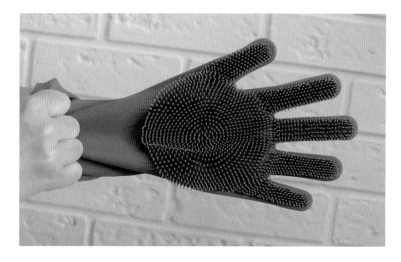

'Magic' silicone dishwashing gloves incorporate a brush on each palm.

Like an inflated balloon, the fingers of the gloves resist the effort to bend them. Astronauts must fight that pressure with every movement of their hand, which is exhausting and sometimes results in injury. Furthermore the joints of the glove are subject to wear that can lead to life-threatening leaks.[22]

Astronauts' hands need to be insulated from extreme temperatures and protected from the vacuum of space, and their gloves have to be strong enough to resist puncture by pieces of space debris, yet flexible enough to allow their fingers to undertake essential tasks.

Aesthetics are unimportant in outer space; functionality is all, for failure could be lethal. For Apollo 11's moon mission in 1969, extravehicular gloves were custom-made to fit Neil Armstrong's hands. They had an inner glove with a pressure layer of neoprene compound and a built-in restraint system; their outer shell was of specially developed metallic Chromel-R fabric with thermal insulation to protect his hands against the extreme heat and cold, and the blue fingertips were made of silicone rubber to provide sensitivity. But their functionality did not end there. Like many terrestrial gloves, they carried a message, though not one of status or propriety or seduction. These were gloves to be read in the most literal of ways and for the most practical of purposes: the left cuff carried a printed checklist reminding Armstrong of the sequence of tasks and procedures he had to complete on the surface of the moon.

It might seem, then, that since the 1960s glove production has been dominated by functionality to the exclusion of beauty, romance, magic and mystery, with gloves no longer serving as personal guarantees of honesty or ownership, or as proof of identity, or as love talismans. But their old cultural symbolism has not vanished entirely.

Gloves once worn by celebrities can fetch dizzying prices at auction, suggesting that their former owners' glamorous identity and allure are felt still to adhere to them, much as saints' gloves were venerated for retaining the sanctity of the hands they

Pair of Russian Sokol spacesuit gloves at the Gagarin Cosmonaut Training Centre, Russia, 2016. Space travel presents special challenges for glove design.

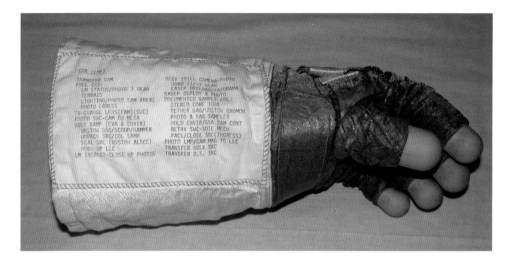

once covered. Strictly functional modern gloves may develop their own mystique too, as is clear from the crowds of museum visitors who come to gaze at gloves that have travelled to outer space and back on the hands of astronauts. Even the Power Glove, an ugly and cumbersome video-game controller launched by the Mattel toy company in 1989, has transcended its original function and developed the aura of a cult object. Designed to allow its wearer to operate Nintendo games by using hand gestures, the Power Glove has come to encapsulate nostalgia for the early days of gaming, and has generated artworks, songs and videos; bands have been named after it; and in 2017 it was the inspiration for a film, *The Power of Glove*.

Although gloves are no longer considered essential everyday wear, luxurious, glamorously flamboyant versions continue to entice. Their striking visual impact is enhanced by clever photography and fashion magazines and online platforms such as Instagram swiftly disseminate their seductive appeal. The young British designer Taylor-Bea Gordon, described in the press as 'the glove lady' and 'the designer behind Instagram's favourite accessory', specializes in making showy, ruffled, diaphanous gloves from deadstock silk organza, and has expressed surprise

Neil Armstrong's extravehicular left glove for the Apollo 11 moon landing mission, 1969. The cuff has a printed checklist of procedures to be completed on the moon.

at the speed with which their images gained wide publicity and popularity: 'I just started posting them on social media and they became quite a thing that people kept requesting: different magazines, stylists and photographers. All of a sudden people were writing about the gloves.'[23]

The major fashion houses in Paris, Milan and New York regularly show eye-catching gloves, designed to accompany couture outfits down the catwalk and, increasingly, celebrities are photographed in stunning versions. The desire for conspicuously adorned hands seems as strong as in the days of lavishly embroidered Renaissance gauntlets.

'Opera Gloves Are Fast Becoming Hollywood's Favorite Accessory,' announced *Vogue* in January 2020:

> Sometimes the look of the moment all comes down to a single item. After the dominance of mini-bags, ugly shoes, and limited-edition sneakers, a new accessory has risen to the forefront: opera gloves . . . It's rare for a piece that hit its peak during the 50s to resonate with millennials and Gen-Z, but the look's current adherents are risk-taking young stars who draw inspiration from the past.

But as the same article points out, these gloves are being worn in new and adventurous ways that pay little heed to the rules of etiquette laid down in old advice manuals. They are emphatically modern, rather than a straightforward imitation of 1950s fashion:

> The new generation has also upended the old rules about when, where, and how gloves should be worn. Emily Post once held that gloves should only be worn with formalwear and that they should cover rings and other jewelry. Don't tell that to Beyoncé, who piled on

Lorraine Schwartz diamonds and emeralds over hers at Diddy's 50th birthday party in December. These days, anything goes, and celebrities are opting for bright colours, unique materials, and plenty of gems to amp up the drama.[24]

Although created to capture the mood of the moment and worn with modern panache, beautifully crafted designer gloves continue to play with many of the old associations that have accrued to gloves over the centuries. Versace's long, tight black nappa leather gloves spell out gloves' traditional amorous connotations in the most literal way, with L-O-V-E picked out in large white letters down the arm. So, too, does a short black leather pair by Agnelle, which has the letters L-O and V-E appliquéed over a scarlet leather heart that is broken or mended as the hands move apart or come together – a playful new variant on the lovers and Cupids that decorated many early nineteenth-century printed gloves, and a nod to their flirtatious language.

Dolce & Gabbana's long black woollen gloves with their enormous ruby-like rhinestones on the fingers hark back to Renaissance gloves, slashed to show off a hand's jewelled rings. The same company's Fall 2014 collection showed strikingly opulent creations for men and women that clearly referenced the famous thirteenth-century gloves of the Holy Roman Emperor and the jewel-studded gloves of medieval prelates. Like them, these ultra-modern gloves were encrusted with seed pearls and jewels, and some had quasi-religious enamel medallions like those of liturgical gloves nestling among the gems. Religious inspiration was also evident in the exquisite single leather gauntlet shown in Alexander McQueen's posthumous 2010 'Angels and Demons' collection, digitally printed with details taken from the famous fifteenth-century Dombild altarpiece in Cologne. The glove's long, flared shape also recalled that of medieval hawking gauntlets, hinting at the designer's passion for falconry.

These men's jewel-encrusted gloves from Dolce & Gabbana's 2014 collection are reminiscent of the 13th-century gloves of the Holy Roman Emperor.

Gloves' old association with magic and mystery lives on, too, and appeals to copywriters as a way of piquing interest in a new style. 'Every so often, something magical happens, and a glove is born that is unlike any other,' says the Amsterdam luxury glove company, Ines, announcing a 'sensational one-piece extreme length corset leather glove . . . for men and women'.[25] But gloves' magical properties are more evident in the re-emergence of the transformative powers traditionally credited to them. Designers exploit their uncanny capacity to blur the boundaries of the human hand and conjure an animal or botanical presence. The elongated, flower-studded gloves shown by Delpozo in Fall 2016 transformed hands and arms into long floral bouquets, as if the wearer were undergoing a strange and beautiful metamorphosis.

And at Burberry Prorsum's Fall 2012 show, unsettling gloves of python skin, dyed a deep yellow and with big, loose scales, looked as if they might have come from the skin of a dragon.

Such superbly crafted, attention-grabbing gloves denote wealth and status quite as much as did the ornate, embroidered, spangled, fringed and perfumed gloves favoured by Renaissance monarchs. Today, Queen Elizabeth II prefers a far simpler style in plain black, white or parchment double-shrunk cotton. Although understated, the gloves, which have been made for her by the Cornelia James workshop for many decades, are nevertheless an important way of projecting the royal image. As James's daughter, Genevieve, who now runs the company, points out:

> The mind's eye picture of the queen is of her sitting in her black limousine and from the corner of the car you see the white-gloved hand waving . . . You never see her without her hat, her handbag or her gloves. Nobody apart from the queen wears gloves all the time. The queen wears gloves all the time because she likes to

Long gloves by the Spanish brand Delpozo transform the wearer's arms into floral bouquets, 2016.

Queen Elizabeth II
wears plain black
cotton gloves on a
visit to Liverpool
in 2012. Gloves
are an essential
part of her royal
image.

and she's the queen. They are part of her integral style
and she's iconic.[26]

What is undeniable is that, whether decorative or functional, gloves still tell stories, as they have always done, and
reflect the desires and preoccupations of the times. Recently, for
example, the luxury glove company Gaspar has responded to
the COVID-19 pandemic by producing water-resistant and fully
washable 'hygiene gloves' in unlined, super-thin leather – an
elegant, if expensive, alternative to the ubiquitous disposable
latex versions.[27]

Many artists, intrigued by gloves' multiple meanings and
messages, turn them into works of art. American artist Laura
Splan has created a ghostly pair of gloves from cosmetic facial
peel, cast from her own hands. All the pores and follicles and
creases of the absent hands are faithfully reproduced in the delicate, translucent sculptures, dissolving the distinction between
hand and glove to suggest a new intimacy. For Splan, 'the vivid
detail of the hand and the implied function of the glove evoke
the metaphor of "slipping into the skin of another".'[28]

Paul Villinski, an artist whose work frequently repurposes discarded materials, is likewise interested in the idea that gloves can let us see into the lives of others. He works with gloves found on the streets of New York, and is particularly sensitive to their imagined histories. To him, these lost gloves retain something of their owners, but also reflect wider fears and vulnerabilities:

> Instantly you wonder: whose was this – their
> sex and age and body type – their laugh? What
> work was done? You begin to construct entire
> identities, for the gloves are replete with memory,
> with personal history. They are almost the hands
> themselves, in ways even more telling . . . They have
> qualities we fear coming to know: carelessly left
> behind, forgotten or discarded, weathered, damaged,
> exhausted and worn through, run over by life,
> homeless. Lost and found. So I bring them into
> the studio and into pieces and give them homes,
> with the others.[29]

More recently, as the COVID-19 pandemic began to affect people's lives, other artists have seen special significance in carelessly abandoned medical gloves. The British photographer Dan Giannopoulos realized that he could document powerful, topical emotions by photographing the rubber gloves he was suddenly finding discarded on the streets of his immediate neighbourhood. Recorded where they lay, the gloves are seen not in relation to individual owners or locality, but to a society in crisis:

> These disposable gloves quickly came to represent
> the sheer scale of the public health crisis . . . [and]
> the paranoia and panic that people are feeling
> under the immense pressure of this invisible killer.

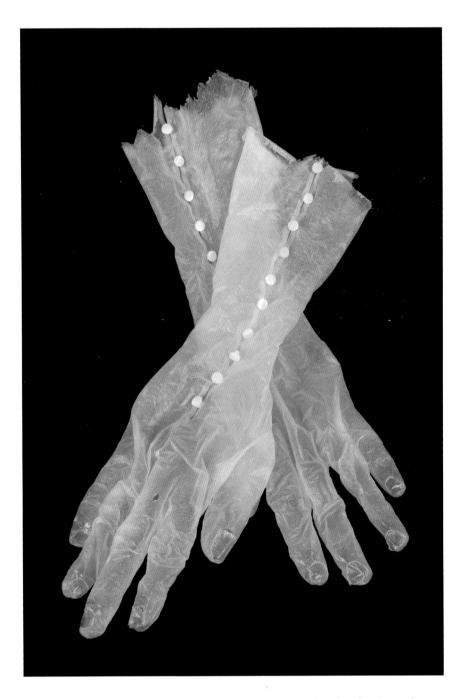

Laura Splan, *Trousseau (Gloves)*, 2009, cosmetic facial peel and mixed media. The work reproduces the creases, pores and follicles of the artist's absent hands.

These discarded gloves also represented, to me, our own virulent impact on the environment. If this small sample is anything to go by then there are hundreds of thousands of these gloves scattered across the empty public spaces of this country.[30]

Let us end this book with one of the most extraordinary and resonant gloves to have been created in recent times: a single chain-mail gauntlet with long, diamond-studded talons, decorated with a graceful flight of diamond-studded birds, and crafted from white gold. Its production took four years and involved four goldsmiths, 21 fittings and 4,290 diamonds.[31] Jointly conceived by the model and artist Daphne Guinness, the jewellery designer Shaun Leane and the fashion designer Alexander McQueen, this astonishing piece was exhibited to the public in July 2011 at an event that took the form of a mock funeral. Like the effigy of a medieval knight on a tomb, Guinness lay motionless, shrouded in veils, with only her hand emerging from the folds, clad in the long, glittering mesh gauntlet. The glove was named 'Contra Mundum' – 'Against the World'.

Describing it as combining 'an armour-like structure with the elegant femininity of a satin evening glove', Leane explained that the piece was inspired by a comment from Guinness about longing for armour to protect her at a crowded social gathering. The glove, which began with a plaster mould of Guinness's forearm so that its white gold links could take on the exact shape of her hand and arm, was designed to embody her anxieties and convey her desire to be armoured against outsiders. As Guinness explained to a journalist in a comment that captures gloves' capacity to protect and to reveal and to conceal, 'It's sort of us against the world. It's about wanting to watch, but not wanting to be seen.'[32]

The glove was a dazzling display of opulence, designed to impress as an aesthetic object and as a feat of craftsmanship.

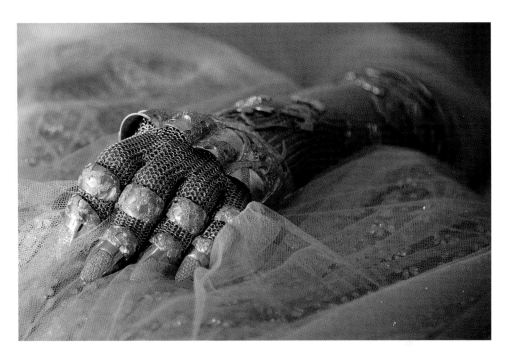

This was fashion and art and armour, troubling and ambiguous, protecting the inner vulnerability of its wearer and exemplifying many of the chameleon-like qualities of a gloved hand. Wearing it, Guinness felt transformed:

> There's a feeling of being amplified. You're augmented in the right sense of the word. It is empowering, and I also feel he [Shaun Leane] is with me. He's my great friend, and it's lovely to know I've got something of his on me, protecting me like an amulet.[33]

Some of the diamonds on the glove had once belonged to her, making her feel as if little pieces of her own history were embedded in it.

Although excessive and impractical and unlike any other glove in existence, the diamond-studded gauntlet encapsulates the qualities of gloves discussed in this book. Like many of them, it is designed to dazzle and impress. It protects. Its fine, silvery mesh closely reproduces the hand within, yet is clearly not a hand. Its flying birds and pointed talons hint that a strange metamorphosis is taking place, and its wearer feels 'amplified' and 'augmented', as if by magic. It is worn as a talisman and as a memento of a loved one. It is both ancient and modern in form, and full of contradictions. Breathtaking in its beauty and extravagance, surreal in its dreamlike strangeness, the *Contra Mundum* gauntlet is, in a sense, the quintessential glove.[34]

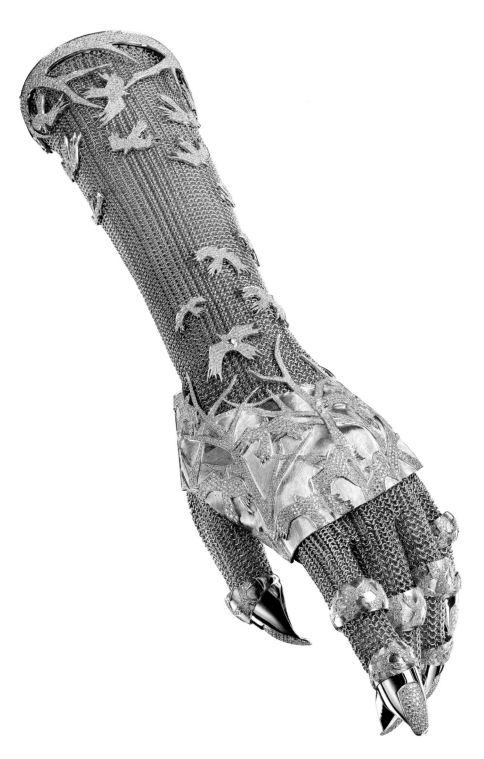

Contra Mundum, a unique white gold and diamond evening glove by Shaun Leane, Daphne Guinness and Alexander McQueen, 2011.

REFERENCES

Introduction

1 Clara Young, 'Give Me Five: The Glove Makes a Comeback', www.ellecanada.com, 14 October 2009.
2 Ibid.
3 See www.inesgloves.com, accessed 9 November 2020.
4 Manuel Rubio, general manager of Causse, quoted in Sarah Shard, 'Gloves Making a Comeback as Alternative Accessory to Brag Bag', http://smh.com.au, 1 November 2007; and in 'Luxury and Ancient Craft Go Hand in Glove in French Town', www.dailystar.com.lb, 21 January 2013.
5 Young, 'Give Me Five'.
6 Marguerite de Navarre, *The Heptameron* [1558], trans. P. A. Chilton (London, 1984), pp. 457–8.
7 *Cambridge Dictionary*, www.dictionary.cambridge.org, accessed 11 November 2020.

ONE: 'Musk-scented, fragrant, invented by Venus': Early Gloves

1 Jean Godard, *Le Gan* (Paris, 1588), p. 11.
2 Xenophon, *Cyropaedia: The Education of Cyrus*, trans. Wayne Ambler (Cornell, NY, 2001), p. 275.
3 Musonius Rufus, in *Musonius Rufus: 'The Roman Socrates'*, trans. Cora Lutz (New Haven, CT, 1949), *Yale Classical Studies*, vol. X, p. 121.

4 Letter 27, to Baebius Macer, in *Letters of Pliny*,
  ed. F.C.T. Bosanquet, trans. William Melmoth
  (Project Gutenberg EBook), www.gutenberg.org.

5 Athenaeus, *The Deipnosophists*, trans. C. D. Yonge
  (London, 1854), Book 12, p. 70.

6 S. Ireland, *Roman Britain: A Sourcebook* [1986]
  (London, 1996), p. 194.

7 See http://curses.csad.ox.ac.uk.

8 Virgil, *The Aeneid of Virgil*, trans. J. W. Mackail
  (London, 1885), Book V, pp. 104–5.

9 Geoffrey Chaucer, *The Canterbury Tales*, trans. Nevill
  Coghill (London, 1962), p. 94.

10 Annemarieke Willemsen, 'Taking Up the Glove: Finds, Uses
  and Meanings of Gloves, Mittens and Gauntlets in Western
  Europe, *c.* AD 1300–1700', *Post-medieval Archaeology*,
  XLIX/1 (2015), p. 4.

11 Godard, *Le Gan*, p. 10.

12 Ibid., p. 8.

13 Guillaume de Lorris and Jean de Meun, *The Romance
  of the Rose*, trans. Charles Dahlberg (Princeton, NJ, 1995),
  p. 38.

14 Henri de Villiers, *Essais historiques sur les modes et la
  toilette françaises* (Paris, 1824), p. 95.

15 *The Song of Roland and Other Poems of Charlemagne*,
  trans. Simon Gaunt and Karen Pratt (Oxford, 2016), p. 13.

16 Ibid., p. 90.

17 Ibid., p. 94.

18 *Sketches from Venetian History*, 2 vols (London, 1832),
  vol. II, pp. 87–8.

19 Françoise de Bonneville, *Le Gant* (Paris, 2007), p. 33.

20 Giles Gossip (pseud.), *Coronation Anecdotes; or, Select and
  Interesting Fragments of English Coronation Ceremonies*
  (London, 1823), pp. 267–9.

21 'Proceedings at the King's Coronation, 23 June 1377',
  www.nationalarchives.gov.uk, accessed 9 November 2020.

22 Thomas Fuller, *The Church History of Britain*, 6 vols
  (Oxford, 1845), vol. I, p. 384. Cited in Peter Stallybrass and

Ann Rosalind Jones, 'Fetishizing the Glove in Renaissance Europe', *Critical Inquiry*, XXVIII/1 (Autumn 2001), p. 116.

23 *The Revelations of Saint Birgitta of Sweden*, trans. Denis Searby (Oxford, 2006), vol. III, p. 111.

24 Bonneville, *Le Gant*, p. 169; Michèle Beaulieu, 'Les Gants liturgiques en France au moyen âge', *Bulletin archéologique du comité des travaux historiques et scientifiques* [1868], new series, IV (Paris, 1969), p. 138, n. 9.

25 See Mary Wellesley, 'This Place is a Pryson', *London Review of Books*, XXXXI/10 (23 May 2019).

26 Ibid., p. 138.

27 Willemsen, 'Taking Up the Glove', p. 24; John S. Ott, *Bishops, Authority and Community in Northwestern Europe, c. 1050–1150* (Cambridge, 2015), p. 72; 'White Gloves or Not White Gloves?', blogs.bl.uk, 19 August 2011.

28 Godard, *Le Gan*, p. 6.

29 'Devotions for a Priest', Beinecke MS461, http://brbl-dl. library.yale.edu.

30 Beaulieu, 'Les Gants liturgiques', p. 142.

31 Elizabeth Coatsworth and Gale Owen-Crocker, *Clothing the Past: Surviving Garments from Early Medieval to Early Modern Western Europe* (Leiden and Boston, MA, 2018), pp. 401, 410.

32 James William Norton-Kyshe, *The Law and Customs Relating to Gloves, Being an Exposition Historically Viewed of Ancient Laws, Customs, and Uses in Respect of Gloves, and of the Symbolism of the Hand and Glove in Judicial Proceedings* (London, 1901), pp. 49–51.

33 William Shakespeare, *Love's Labour's Lost*, in *The Complete Works of William Shakespeare*, ed. John Dover Wilson (London, 1980), p. 187.

34 Norton-Kyshe, *Law and Customs*, p. 26.

35 Ibid., pp. 33–4.

36 Cited ibid., p. 36.

37 Leopold Wagner, *Manners, Customs and Observances: Their Origin and Signification* (London, 1895), pp. 117–18.

38 'Merrymaking Begins as the Glove Is Raised at Axminster', *East Devon* 24, 22 June 2017.

39 'Historical Collection: 1631', www.british-history.ac.uk.

40 Wang Xiangwei, 'Corruption Trials Expose Roles of the "White Gloves" Who Manage the Ill-gotten Gains', www.scmp.com, 9 September 2013.

41 Herodotus, *The Histories*, trans. Aubrey de Sélincourt (London, 1968), p. 385.

42 Cited in Hugh F. Martindale, *A Familiar Analysis of the Calendar of the Church of England* (London, 1830), pp. 7–8.

43 William Cecil (Lord Burghley), *A Collection of State Papers, Relating to Affairs in the Reigns of Henry VIII, Edward VI, Mary and Elizabeth*, ed. Samuel Haynes (London, 1740), p. 368.

44 Christopher Marlowe, *The Massacre at Paris*, in *The Complete Works of Christopher Marlowe*, ed. Fredson Bowers, 2 vols (Cambridge, 1981), vol. I, p. 365.

45 Evelyn Welch, 'Art on the Edge: Hair and Hands in Renaissance Italy', *Renaissance Studies*, XXIII/3 (June 2009), pp. 261–2.

46 Patricia Wardle, *Embroidery Most Sumptuously Wrought: Dutch Designs in the Metropolitan Museum of Art* (New York, 2010), n.p., www.books.google.co.uk, accessed 11 November 2020.

47 Cited in Alan H. Nelson, *Monstrous Adversary: The Life of Edward de Vere, 17th Earl of Oxford* (Liverpool, 2003), p. 180.

48 Cited in Elizabeth Stone, *Chronicles of Fashion, from the Time of Queen Elizabeth to the Present Day* (London, 1846), vol. I, p. 412.

49 Helen Rawson, *600 Years in the Making: Highlights from the Museum Collections of the University of St Andrews* (London, 2016), p. 14; Marieke de Winkel, *Fashion and Fancy: Dress and Meaning in Rembrandt's Paintings* (Amsterdam, 2006), p. 87.

50 *Dealings with the Dead, by a Sexton of the Old School* (Boston, MA, 1856), vol. I, p. 92.

51 Steven Bullock and Sheila McIntyre, 'The Handsome Tokens of a Funeral: Glove-giving and the Large Funeral in Eighteenth-century New England', *William and Mary Quarterly*, LXIX/2 (April 2012), p. 321.

52 See ibid., pp. 305–46.

53 Ibid., pp. 323–4.

54 Ibid., p. 317.

55 Samuel Pepys, *The Diary of Samuel Pepys*, ed. Robert Latham and William Matthews, 11 vols (London, 1970–83), vol. IX, p. 427.

56 Ibid., vol. IV, p. 427.

57 Ibid., vol. III, p. 297.

58 Ibid., vol. II, pp. 38, 40.

59 Ibid., vol. IV, p. 218; vol. VIII, p. 202.

60 Ibid., vol. VII, p. 29.

61 Ibid., vol. VIII, p. 100; vol. V, p. 264.

62 Ibid., vol. VIII, p. 425.

63 Ibid., vol. IX, p. 412.

64 Ibid., vol. VIII, p. 303.

65 'Venice: July 1618, 16–31', www.british-history.ac.uk, accessed 10 November 2020.

TWO: Tranks, Forgits and Quirks: Making Gloves

1 Cited in William Hull, *The History of the Glove Trade, with the Customs Connected with the Glove: to which are annexed some observations on the policy of the trade between England and France, and its operation on the agricultural and manufacturing interests* (London, 1834), p. 52.

2 Ibid., p. 53.

3 René de Lespinasse, *Les Métiers et corporations de la ville de Paris: XIVe–XVIIIe siècles* (Paris, 1897), vol. III, p. 605.

4 Ibid.

5 Françoise de Bonneville, *Le Gant* (Paris, 2007), p. 43.

6 Lespinasse, *Les Métiers et corporations*, p. 606.

7 Cited in H. Southern, ed., *The Retrospective Review*, second series (1827), vol. I, p. 226.

8 Fernando de Rojas, *Celestina*, trans. Peter Bush (London, 2009), p. 179; Michel de Montaigne, *Essais*, Book 1, ch. 55, in *Oeuvres complètes* (Paris, 1967), pp. 137–8.

9 Holly Dugan, *The Ephemeral History of Perfume: Scent and Sense in Early Modern England* (Baltimore, MD, 2011), p. 132.

10 Ben Jonson, *The Alchemist*, in *Four Plays* (London, 2014), p. 389.

11 Gervase Markham, *Countrey Contentments; or, The English Huswife, containing the Inward and Outward Vertues which ought to be in a Compleate Woman* (London, 1623), p. 142.

12 See www.guerlain.com, accessed 10 November 2020.

13 Hull, *History of the Glove Trade*, p. 11.

14 *Patrimoine urbain de la ganterie grenobloise* (Grenoble, 2017), n.p.

15 *Bulletin de la société de statistique, des sciences naturelles et des arts industriels du département de l'Isère* (Grenoble, 1851), pp. 201–8.

16 John Banks, *Reminiscences of Smugglers and Smuggling* (London, 1873), p. 3.

17 Sarah Murden, '18th Century Tax on Gloves', www.georgianera.wordpress.com, accessed 10 November 2020.

18 *Sherborne and Taunton Journal*, 21 May 1829, cited in Bob Osborn, 'Leather and Gloving in Yeovil', www.yeovilhistory.info.gloving-intro, accessed 10 November 2020.

19 Hull, *History of the Glove Trade*, pp. 54–5.

20 Ibid., p. 56.

21 Edouard Rey, *Xavier Jouvin* (Paris, 1868).

22 Ibid., p. 110.

23 *Bulletin de la société de statistique*, pp. 203, 205.

24 *Exposition universelle de 1867: Rapports du jury
   international* (Paris, 1868), vol. IV, pp. 330–31.
   See also Michel Alcan et al., *Visite à l'exposition
   universelle de Paris en 1855* (Paris, 1855), p. 54.

25 Alfred Picard, *Exposition universelle internationale de 1900
   à Paris: Le bilan d'un siècle, 1801–1900* (Paris, 1906), vol. IV,
   p. 436.

26 Ibid.

27 *Strawbridge and Clothier's Quarterly*, II/1 (1883), p. 27.

28 *Le Génie industriel* (1851), vol. I, pp. 405–6 and plate 24.

29 Patent no. GB140908A, https://worldwide.espacenet.com,
   accessed 10 November 2020.

30 *Exposition universelle de 1878: Rapports du jury
   international* (Paris, 1880), p. 304.

31 *Etudes sur l'exposition universelle de 1878: Annales et
   archives de l'industrie au XIXe siècle* (Paris, 1878), vol. IV,
   p. 341.

32 Mrs Henry Wood, *Mrs Halliburton's Troubles*, 20th edn
   (London, 1888), p. 134.

33 Ibid., p. 97.

34 Ibid., p. 121.

35 Ibid., p. 96.

36 Sir Walter Scott, *The Fair Maid of Perth; or, St Valentine's
   Day*, in *The Waverley Novels*, 25 vols (Edinburgh, 1891),
   vol. XXII, p. 19.

37 Ibid., p. 365.

38 Ibid., p. 71.

39 Ibid., pp. 32, 315.

40 Ibid., pp. 65–6.

41 Ibid., p. 66.

42 Ibid., p. 72.

43 Elie Berthet, *Le Gouffre* (Paris, 1872), pp. 57, 111–13.

44 Ibid., pp. 112–13.

45 Alison Matthews David, *Fashion Victims: The Dangers
   of Dress Past and Present* (London, 2015), p. 79.

46 Patent for glove-drying machine by John J. Jenkins (1917),
   Canadian Patent Document 180191.

47 Louis Rouvier, *Des Altérations professionnelles des ouvriers gantiers et palissonneurs, envisagées au point de vue de l'identité* (Paris, 1883), p. 57.

48 See www.sermonetagloves.it, accessed 10 November 2020.

49 See www.dentsgloves.com, accessed 10 November 2020.

50 See www.topglove.com, accessed 10 November 2020.

51 Philip Roth, *American Pastoral* (London, 1997), p. 221.

52 Ibid., p. 67.

53 Ibid., p. 66.

54 Ibid.

55 Ibid., p. 348.

56 Ibid., pp. 224–5.

57 Ibid., pp. 26–7.

58 Ibid., p. 349.

59 Ibid., pp. 345–6.

60 Ibid., pp. 421–2.

THREE: 'Tear at the Thumb, Troubles to Come':
The Language of Gloves

1 *The Institutio Oratoria of Quintilian*, trans. H. E. Butler (Cambridge, MA, 1920), vol. IV, pp. 289–91.

2 Charles Blanc, *L'Art dans la parure et dans le vêtement* (Paris, 1875), p. 179.

3 Ibid., p. 178.

4 Huntington Digital Library, call mark 18343, hdl. huntington.org.

5 George Dalgarno, *Didascalocophus; or, The Deaf and Dumb Man's Tutor* (Oxford, 1680), p. 88.

6 'Talking Gloves', www.nineteenthcenturydisability.org, accessed 10 November 2020.

7 Carol Padden and Tom Humphries, *Deaf in America: Voices from a Culture* (Harvard, MA, 1990), p. 53.

8 Timothy Revell, 'Glove Turns Sign Language into Text for Real-time Translation', www.newscientist.com, 12 July 2017; Michael Scaturro, 'This Glove Could Help

Deaf-blind People Communicate with Anyone, Anywhere',
www.theatlantic.com, 26 June 2013.

9 Madeleine Delpierre, *Dress in France in the Eighteenth
Century*, trans. Caroline Beamish (New Haven, CT, 1997),
p. 41.

10 Vicomte de Marennes, *Manuel de l'homme et de la femme
comme il faut* (Paris, 1855), p. 70.

11 'Black Athletes Make Silent Protest', www.bbc.co.uk,
17 October 1968.

12 Iris Origo, *The Merchant of Prato* (New York, 1957), p. 290.

13 Evelyn Welch, 'Art on the Edge: Hair and Hands in
Renaissance Italy', *Renaissance Studies*, XXIII/3
(June 2009), p. 262.

14 Jean-Baptiste de la Salle, *Règles de la bienséance et
de la civilité chrétiennes* [1703] (Rheims, 1736), p. 61.

15 G. Guenot-Lecointe, *Physiologie du gant* (Paris, 1841),
pp. 66, 84.

16 Ibid., p. 72.

17 Ibid., p. 84.

18 Ibid.

19 Madame Emile de Girardin, *Lettres parisiennes*, 4 vols
(Paris, 1857), vol. I, p. 50.

20 Gustave Flaubert, *Correspondance*, ed. J. Bruneau and
Y. Leclerc, 5 vols (Paris, 1973–2007), vol. I, p. 355.

21 Marennes, *Manuel de l'homme*, p. 70.

22 Girardin, *Lettres parisiennes*, vol. II, p. 261.

23 Samuel R. Wells, *How to Behave: A Pocket Manual of
Republican Etiquette, and Guide to Correct Personal
Habits, Embracing an Exposition of the Principles
of Good Manners* (New York, 1887), p. 38.

24 George Routledge, *Routledge's Manual of Etiquette*
(London, 1875), p. 14.

25 Guenot-Lecointe, *Physiologie*, p. 85. See also ibid.,
p. 109: 'One can tell how distinguished a man is by
the shade of his gloves.'

26 Bertall, *La Comédie de notre temps: Études au crayon
et à la plume. La civilité, les habitudes, les moeurs, les*

costumes, les manières et les manies de notre époque,
3 vols (Paris, 1874–76), vol. I, p. 58.

27 Blanc, *L'Art dans la parure*, pp. 260–61.

28 Madame Celnart, *Manuel des dames, ou l'art de l'élégance,
sous le rapport de la toilette, des honneurs de la maison, des
plaisirs, des occupations agréables* (Paris, 1833), pp. 135–6.

29 Anon., *The Habits of Good Society: A Handbook of
Etiquette for Ladies and Gentlemen* (London, 1859), p. 118.

30 Guenot-Lecointe, *Physiologie*, p. 86.

31 Blanc, *L'Art dans la parure*, p. 178.

32 Guenot-Lecointe, *Physiologie*, pp. 85–6; Bertall, *Comédie*,
vol. I, p. 58.

33 Henry Lunettes, *The American Gentleman's Guide
to Politeness and Fashion; or, Familiar Letters to his
Nephews* (New York, 1860), p. 37.

34 Routledge, *Routledge's Manual*, pp. 157–8.

34 Ibid., pp. 14, 163.

35 Celnart, *Manuel des dames*, p. 222.

36 For example, Blanc, *L'Art dans la parure*, p. 259;
Guenot-Lecointe, *Physiologie*, p. 85.

37 Émile Zola, *Au Bonheur des dames* [1883], ed. Henri
Mitterand (Paris, 1980), p. 137.

38 Eliza Leslie, *The Ladies' Guide to True Politeness and
Perfect Manners* [1837] (Philadelphia, PA, 1864), p. 83.

39 Cora Linn Daniels and C. M. Stevans, eds, *Encyclopedia
of Superstitions, Folklore, and the Occult Sciences
of the World* (Honolulu, HI, 2003), vol. I, p. 456.

40 Clarisse Juranville, *Le Savoir-faire et le savoir-vivre dans
les diverses circonstances de la vie: Guide pratique de la vie
usuelle à l'usage des jeunes filles* (Paris, 1879), p. 41.

41 I am grateful to Heather Glen for sharing this memory.

42 Champfleury, *Contes d'automne* (Paris, 1854), p. 209.

43 Florence Hartley, *The Ladies' Book of Etiquette and
Manual of Politeness* (Boston, MA, 1860), p. 174.

44 Honoré de Balzac, *Traité de la vie élégante*, in *La Comédie
humaine*, ed. Pierre-Georges Castex (Paris, 1976–81),
vol. XII, p. 257.

45 Routledge, *Routledge's Manual*, p. 14.

46 Blanche Staffe, *Mes Secrets* (Paris, 1896), p. 131.

47 See, for example, Celnart, *Manuel des dames*, pp. 222–3; Juranville, *Le Savoir-faire*, p. 175.

48 Blanche Staffe, *Usages du monde: Règles du savoir-vivre dans la société moderne*, 24th edn (Paris, 1891), p. 71.

49 Guenot-Lecointe, *Physiologie*, pp. 111–13.

50 Flaubert, *Correspondance*, vol. III, p. 192.

51 Marennes, *Manuel de l'homme*, p. 69.

52 Bertall, *Comédie*, vol. I, p. 58.

53 Louise Colet, *Ces Petits Messieurs* (Paris, 1869), p. 83.

54 Routledge, *Routledge's Manual*, p. 182.

55 Guenot-Lecointe, *Physiologie*, pp. 84–5.

56 Anon., *Etiquette for Ladies and Gentlemen* (London, 1876), p. 14.

57 Louise d'Alq, *Notes d'une mère: Cours d'éducation maternelle* (Paris, 1883), pp. 293–4.

58 James Huneker, *Franz Liszt* (New York, 1911), pp. 256–7, 298.

59 Cecil B. Hartley, *The Gentlemen's Book of Etiquette and Manual of Politeness* (Boston, MA, 1860), p. 96; Wells, *How to Behave*, p. 106; Hartley, *The Gentlemen's Book*, pp. 193–4.

60 Ibid.

61 Wells, *How to Behave*, p. 80.

62 Arthur Martine, *Martine's Hand-book of Etiquette, and Guide to True Politeness* (New York, 1866), p. 132.

63 Lunettes, *American Gentleman's Guide*, p. 37.

64 Wells, *How to Behave*, p. 101.

65 Hartley, *The Gentlemen's Book*, p. 96.

66 Martine, *Martine's Hand-book*, p. 69.

67 Wells, *How to Behave*, pp. 92, 89.

68 Leslie, *Ladies' Guide*, p. 34.

69 Anon., *Manners and Rules of Good Society by a Member of the Aristocracy*, 38th edn (London, 1916), pp. 116, 137.

70 Anon., *The Habits of Good Society*, p. 154.

71 Patent no GB189419082A, https://worldwide.espacenet.com, accessed 10 November 2020.

72 Marennes, *Manuel de l'homme*, p. 69.

73 Gustave Flaubert, *L'Education sentimentale* [1869], ed. P. M. Wetherill (Paris, 1984), pp. 59, 91.

74 James Joyce, *The Dubliners* [1914] (London, 1996), p. 160.

75 Charles Dickens, *Bleak House*, in *The Works of Charles Dickens*, 21 vols (London, 1901), vol. XI, p. 461.

76 Thomas Hardy, *Tess of the d'Urbervilles* [1891] (London, 2008), p. 372.

77 Ibid., pp. 387–8.

78 Mrs Henry Wood, *Mrs Halliburton's Troubles*, 20th edn (London, 1888), p. 245.

79 Otto Ludwig [pseud. of Emil von Puttkammer], *The Dead Man of St Anne's Chapel*, in *Early German and Austrian Detective Fiction: An Anthology* [1839], trans. Mary W. Tannert and Henry Kratz (Jefferson, NC, and London, 1999), p. 56.

80 Ibid., p. 62.

81 Flaubert, *Correspondance*, vol. II, p. 538.

82 Ibid., p. 520.

83 Gustave Flaubert, *Les Mémoires d'un fou*, in *Oeuvres de jeunesse*, ed. Claudine Gothot-Mersch and Guy Sagnes (Paris, 2001), p. 470.

84 Gustave Flaubert, *Carnets de travail*, ed. P. M. de Biasi (Paris, 1988), p. 234.

FOUR: 'Fashioned by the Craft of Devils, and with Skins of the Dragon': Magical Gloves

1 *Life*, XXXVII/19 (8 November 1954), p. 59.

2 Advertisement for VY–5011, www.vivamachine.com.cn, accessed 10 November 2020.

3 François Rabelais, *Gargantua*, in *Oeuvres complètes* (Paris, 1962), vol. I, p. 39, n. 1.

4 *The Story of Beowulf*, trans. Ernest J. B. Kirtlan (London, 1913), p. 128.

5 John Lindow, *Swedish Legends and Folktales* (Berkeley, CA, 1978), pp. 126–7.

6 Cited in Holly Dugan, *The Ephemeral History of Perfume: Scent and Sense in Early Modern England* (Baltimore, MD, 2011), p. 126.

7 Thorliefur Gudmundsson Repp, *A Historical Treatise on Trial by Jury, Wager of Law, and other Co-ordinate Forensic Institutions, Formerly in Use in Scandinavia and Iceland* (Edinburgh, 1832), pp. 14–15.

8 Geoffrey Chaucer, *The Canterbury Tales*, trans. Nevill Coghill (London, 1962), p. 258.

9 'Presentations', www.saintgianna.org, accessed 10 November 2020.

10 Nathaniel Hawthorne, *The Scarlet Letter* [1850] (Boston, MA, 1878), p. 191.

11 Walter Scott, *Minstrelsy of the Scottish Border* [1802], 3rd edn (London, 1806), vol. III, pp. 34–5.

12 Hans Christian Andersen, 'The Marsh King's Daughter', in *Fairy Tales from Hans Christian Andersen* (London, 1915), p. 229.

13 *The Story of the Volsungs*, trans. William Morris and Eirikr Magnusson (London, 1888), ch. 7.

14 Richard Schickel, *The Disney Version: The Life, Times, Art and Commerce of Walt Disney* (New York, 1968), p. 17.

15 'Messages across Time and Space: Inupiat Drawings from the 1890s at Columbia University – a digital companion to an exhibition at the Center for the Study of Ethnicity and Race', https://edblogs.columbia.edu/AHISG4862_001_2015_1/sample-page/curatorial-statement.

16 J. K. Rowling, *Harry Potter and the Order of the Phoenix* (London, 2003), p. 22.

17 Cora Linn Daniels and C. M. Stevans, eds, *Encyclopedia of Superstitions, Folklore, and the Occult Sciences of the World*, 3 vols (Honolulu, HI, 2003), vol. I, pp. 455–6.

18 *Annals of Ireland* [1341], cited in *Dublin Penny Journal*, I/51 (15 June 1833), p. 407.

19 See Neil Thomas, *'Diu Crône' and the Medieval Arthurian Cycle* (Cambridge, 2002), pp. 6, 77.

20 Roald Dahl, *The Witches* (London, 2010), pp. 30–31.

21 Elizabeth Bowen, 'Hand in Glove', in *The Collected Stories of Elizabeth Bowen* (London, 1985), p. 768.

22 Ibid., pp. 774–5.

23 *County Folklore: Leicestershire and Rutland*, ed. Charles J. Billson, I/3 (London, 1895), pp. 47–8.

24 Ernest W. Baughman, *Type and Motif-Index of the Folktales of England and North America* (The Hague, 1966), p. 220.

25 W. B. Yeats, 'Dreams That Have No Moral', in *The Collected Works in Verse and Prose*, 8 vols (Stratford, 1908), vol. V, pp. 185–6.

26 *The Younger Edda: Also Called Snorre's Edda; or, The Prose Edda*, trans. R. B. Anderson (Chicago, IL, 1901), pp. 116–17.

27 Reginetta Haboucha, *King Solomon and the Golden Fish: Tales from the Sephardic Tradition* (Detroit, MI, 2004), p. 52, n. 2.

28 Chris Michaud, 'Michael Jackson's Glove Sells for $350,000 at Auction', www.reuters.com, 23 November 2009.

FIVE: 'Place this Glove neere thy Heart':
Gloves and Loves

1 Jean Godard, *Le Gan* (Paris, 1588), p. 6.

2 Clara Young, 'Give Me Five: The Glove Makes a Comeback', www.ellecanada.com, 14 October 2009.

3 Cora Linn Daniels and C. M. Stevans, eds, *Encyclopedia of Superstitions, Folklore, and the Occult Sciences of the World*, 3 vols (Honolulu, HI, 2003), vol. I, p. 455.

4 Ibid., p. 456.

5 *Life*, 24 April 1950, p. 17.

6 Sagi Shiffer, 'Gloves vs Mittens: Side by Side Comparison', 29 January 2017, www.glovesmag.com.

7 John Brand, *Observations on Popular Antiquities Chiefly Illustrating the Origin of our Vulgar Customs, Ceremonies and Superstitions*, ed. H. Ellis (London, 1813), vol. II, p. 55.

8   J. R. Smith, *Popular Rhymes and Nursery Tales: A Sequel to the Nursery Rhymes of England* (London, 1849), p. 250.

9   'The Golden Glove', National Library of Scotland Crawford EB 3371, https://digital.nls.uk.

10 See, for example, Laurence Sterne, *A Sentimental Journey Through France and Italy*, ed. Tim Parnell and Ian Jack (Oxford, 2003), pp. 96–9.

11 John Reynolds, *Dolarnys Primrose; or, The First Part of the Passionate Hermit* (London, 1816), n.p.

12 Jonquil O'Reilly, 'Gloves: Useful Symbols', www.sothebys.com, 13 November 2015.

13 Alphonse Karr, *Le Chemin le plus court* (Paris, 1860), p. 8.

14 Cited in P. E. Cunnington and C. Lucas, *Costume for Births, Marriages and Deaths* (New York, 1972), p. 67.

15 Robert Herrick, 'To the Maids, To Walk Abroad', in *Works of Robert Herrick*, ed. Alftred Pollard (London, 1891), vol. III, pp. 15–16.

16 Brand, *Observations*, pp. 55–6.

17 Charles Dickens, *All the Year Round* (London, 1863), vol. IX, p. 427.

18 Ibid.

19 See Patricia Wardle, *Embroidery Most Sumptuously Wrought: Dutch Designs in the Metropolitan Museum of Art* (New York, 2010), n.p., www.books.google.co.uk, accessed 11 November 2020.

20 *The Barrier Miner*, 31 May 1919, p. 7.

21 Evald Tang Kristensen, *Folk and Fairy Tales from Denmark: Oral Tradition Revisited*, trans. Stephen Badman (2015), vol. I, p. 350 ff.

22 Richard Barnfield, Sonnet XIV, in *Poems of Richard Barnfield*, ed. George Klawitter (New York, Lincoln, Shanghai, 2005), p. 105.

23 Ibid.

24 Juan Luis Vives, *The Education of a Christian Woman: A Sixteenth-century Manual*, ed. and trans. Charles Fantazzi (Chicago, IL, and London, 2000), p. 128.

25 Baldassare Castiglione, *The Book of the Courtier* [1528], trans. Leonard Eckstein Opdycke (New York, 1903), p. 55.

26 See Christopher Martin, 'The Breast and Belly of a Queen: Elizabeth After Tilbury', *Early Modern Women: An Interdisciplinary Journal*, II (Fall 2007), p. 5.

27 Thomas Hardy, *The Woodlanders* [1887], ed. Dale Kramer (Oxford, 1981), p. 205.

28 Richard von Krafft-Ebing, *Psychopathia Sexualis* [1886] (Philadelphia, PA, and London, 1892), p. 161.

29 John Cleland, *Fanny Hill; or, Memoirs of a Woman of Pleasure* (London, 1985), p. 190.

30 Sonnet 199, *The Poetry of Petrarch*, trans. and intro. David Young (New York, 2004), p. 148.

31 Sonnets 200 and 201, ibid., p. 149.

32 Théophile Gautier, *Une Larme du diable* [1839], 3rd edn (Paris, 1845), p. 71.

33 Edmond de Goncourt, *Chérie* (Paris, 1884), p. 220.

34 Gustave Flaubert, *Correspondance*, ed. J. Bruneau and Y. Leclerc, 5 vols (Paris, 1973–2007), vol. I, pp. 298–9.

35 Eva Giloi, *Monarchy, Myth and Material Culture in Germany, 1750–1950* (Cambridge, 2011), p. 23.

36 Philip Sidney, *The Old Arcadia* (Oxford, 1999), pp. 148–9.

37 Wilkie Collins, *No Name* [1862], ed. Virginia Blain (Oxford, 1998), pp. 416–17.

38 Jean Godard, *Le Gan* (Paris, 1588), p. 9.

39 Barnabe Barnes, Sonnet LXIII, in *Parthenophil and Parthenope* [1593] (Birmingham, 1882), p. 377.

40 William Shakespeare, *Romeo and Juliet*, in *The Complete Works of William Shakespeare*, ed. John Dover Wilson (London, 1980), p. 788.

41 Gustav Ungerer, *A Spaniard in Elizabethan England: The Correspondence of Antonio Pérez's Exile* (London, 1974), vol. I, p. 199.

42 Gordon Williams, *A Dictionary of Sexual Language and Imagery in Shakespearean and Stuart Literature* (London and Atlantic Highlands, NJ, 1964), vol. II, pp. 603–4.

43 John V. Fleming, *The Roman de la Rose: A Study in Allegory and Iconography* (Princeton, NJ, 1969), p. 85.

44 Alphonse Karr, *Clothilde* (Paris, 1891), p. 227.

45 François Coppée, *Promenades et intérieurs*, in *Oeuvres complètes* (Paris, 1891), p. 334; Guy de Maupassant, *Fort comme la mort* [1889] (Paris, 1965), p. 14.

46 Gustave Flaubert, *Madame Bovary* MSS, in *Brouillons* [Drafts], vol. II, fol. 161; and *Plans et scénarios*, fol. 19, www.flaubert.univ-rouen.fr, accessed 11 November 2020.

47 Giorgio de Chirico, 'Zeuxis the Explorer' [April 1918], trans. S. Heim, *Metaphysical Art*, 14/16 (2016), p. 54.

48 André Breton, 'Manifeste du surréalisme' [1924], in *Manifestes du surréalisme* (Paris, 1985), p. 44.

49 André Breton, *Nadja* (Paris, 1964), pp. 64–5.

50 Brian Sewell, 'The Glove that Changed Guernica', *Evening Standard*, 8 May 2009.

51 Francis Beaumont and John Fletcher, *The Scornful Lady* (London, 1733), p. 34.

52 Margaret Scott, 'Glove', in *The Black Swans* (Hobart, 1985), at www.poetrylibrary.edu.au, accessed 11 November 2020. Quoted with permission from HarperCollins Publishers Australia Pty Limited.

SIX: Archers, Artists and Astronauts: Functions Old and New

1 Blanche Staffe, *Usages du monde: Règles du savoir-vivre dans la société moderne*, 24th edn (Paris, 1891), p. 337.

2 Bertall, *La Comédie de notre temps: Études au crayon et à la plume. La civilité, les habitudes, les moeurs, les costumes, les manières et les manies de notre époque*, 3 vols (Paris, 1874–76), vol. I, p. 58.

3 George Eliot, *Middlemarch* [1871] (London, 1994), pp. 288, 793.

4 Virginia Woolf, 'Mrs Dalloway in Bond Street', in *The Complete Shorter Ficton of Virginia Woolf*, ed. Susan Dick (London, 1985), pp. 146, 153.

5 Virginia Woolf, *Mrs Dalloway*, ed. David Bradshaw (Oxford, 2008), pp. 71–2.

6 Ibid., p. 72.

7 Kayser Glove Adverts [1939–43], www.ghostofthedoll. co.uk, accessed 11 November 2020.

8 *Life*, 7 January 1946, p. 63.

9 *Life*, 19 March 1951, p. 153.

10 Lani Russell, *Sociology for Health Professionals* (Los Angeles, CA, London, New Delhi, 2014).

11 See www.terracycle.com/en-GB/brigades/gloves.

12 Antoine de Pluvinel, *Le Maneige Royal; or, L'Instruction du Roy en L'exercice de Monter à Cheval* [1623], trans. Hilda Nelson (Franktown, VA, 2015), n.p.

13 Gary Lineker, *The Times Magazine*, 7 September 2019, p. 13.

14 Rule 3.04, Official Baseball Rules, www.umpirebible.com, accessed 11 November 2020.

15 Cited in Jim Morrison, 'Baseball's Glove Man', www.smithsonian.com, 12 September 2011.

16 Dorothy Levitt, *The Woman and the Car: A Chatty Little Handbook for All Women Who Motor or Who Want to Motor* (London and New York, 1909), pp. 27–30.

17 Alice Gordenker, 'White Gloves', www.japantimes.co.jp, 19 March 2013.

18 Cited in interview by Emma Foreman, '5 Minutes with . . . Gizelle Renee', www.wolfandbadger.com, accessed 11 November 2020.

19 See www.store.ferrari.com, accessed 11 November 2020.

20 Cited in Deborah Jaffé, *Ingenious Women: From Tincture of Saffron to Flying Machines* (Stroud, 2003), pp. 93–4.

21 See www.mimugloves.com, accessed 11 November 2020.

22 'Astronaut Glove Challenge', www.nasa.gov, accessed 11 November 2020.

23 Cited in Zoe Kendall, 'Meet the Designer behind Instagram's Favourite Accessory', *i-D*, 18 May 2020.

24 Janelle Okwodu, 'Opera Gloves Are Fast Becoming Hollywood's Favorite Accessory', www.vogue.com.au, 7 February 2020.

25 See www.inesgloves.com, accessed 11 November 2020.
26 Sophie Hamilton, 'The Queen's Glove Maker Reveals Why Her Majesty Always Wears the Chic Accessory', www.hellomagazine.com, 3 March 2020.
27 See www.gaspargloves.com, accessed 11 November 2020.
28 See www.laurasplan.com/gloves, accessed 11 November 2020.
29 Paul Villinski, 'On Glove Works', www.paulvillinski.com, accessed 11 November 2020.
30 'Coronavirus: Discarded Disposable Gloves on the Street', www.bbc.co.uk, 7 April 2020.
31 Stephanie Sporn, 'Daphne Guinness and the Diamond-covered Glove that She Almost Destroyed', www.sothebys.com, 20 November, 2017.
32 Sheryl Garratt, 'Daphne Guinness's Glove Story', *Telegraph*, 25 June 2011.
33 Cited in Sporn, 'Daphne Guinness'.
34 In 2017 the *Contra Mundum* glove was sold for around £234,000.

BIBLIOGRAPHY

Anon., *The Habits of Good Society: A Handbook of Etiquette for Ladies and Gentlemen* (London, 1859)

Beaulieu, Michèle, 'Les Gants liturgiques en France au moyen âge', *Bulletin archéologique du comité des travaux historiques et scientifiques*, new series, fasc. 4 [1868] (Paris, 1969), pp. 137–53

Beck, S. William, *Gloves, Their Annals and Associations: A Chapter of Trade and Social History* (London, 1883)

Bonneville, Françoise de, *Le Gant* (Paris, 2007)

Bullock, Steven, and Sheila McIntyre, 'The Handsome Tokens of a Funeral: Glove-giving and the Large Funeral in Eighteenth-century New England', *William and Mary Quarterly*, LXIX/2 (April 2012), pp. 305–46

Coatsworth, Elizabeth, and Gale Owen-Crocker, *Clothing the Past: Surviving Garments from Early Medieval to Early Modern Western Europe* (Leiden and Boston, MA, 2018)

Cumming, Valerie, *Gloves* (London, 1988)

Dugan, Holly, *The Ephemeral History of Perfume: Scent and Sense in Early Modern England* (Baltimore, MD, 2011)

Edwards, Isabel M., *Practical Glove Making* (London, 1929)

Guenot-Lecointe, G., *Physiologie du gant* (Paris, 1841)

Hartley, Cecil B., *The Gentlemen's Book of Etiquette and Manual of Politeness* (Boston, MA, 1860)

Hartley, Florence, *The Ladies' Book of Etiquette and Manual of Politeness* (Boston, MA, 1860)

Hull, William, *The History of the Glove Trade, with the Customs Connected with the Glove: to which are annexed some observations on the policy of the trade between England and France, and its operation on the agricultural and manufacturing interests* (London, 1834)

Hutchings-Goetz, Tracey, 'The Glove as Fetish Object in Eighteenth-century Fiction and Culture', *Eighteenth-century Fiction*, XXXI/2 (Winter 2019), pp. 317–42

Norton-Kyshe, James William, *The Law and Customs Relating to Gloves, Being an Exposition Historically Viewed of Ancient Laws, Customs, and Uses in Respect of Gloves, and of the Symbolism of the Hand and Glove in Judicial Proceedings* (London, 1901)

O'Rourke Boyle, Marjorie, 'Coquette at the Cross? Magdalen in the Master of the Bartholomew Altar's Deposition at the Louvre', *Zeitschrift für Kunstgeschichte*, LIX/4 (1996), pp. 573–7

Redwood, Mike, *Gloves and Glove-making* (London, 2016)

Rey, Edouard, *Xavier Jouvin* (Paris, 1868)

Roth, Philip, *American Pastoral* (London, 1998)

Routledge, George, *Routledge's Manual of Etiquette* (London, 1875)

Schulz, T. E., 'The Woodstock Glove Industry', in *Oxoniensia* (Oxford, 1938), vol. III, pp. 139–52

Staffe, Blanche, *Usages du monde: Règles du savoir-vivre dans la société moderne*, 24th edn (Paris, 1891)

Stallybrass, Peter, and Ann Rosalind Jones, 'Fetishizing the Glove in Renaissance Europe, *Critical Inquiry*, XXVIII/1 (Autumn 2001), pp. 114–32

Wells, Samuel R., *How to Behave: A Pocket Manual of Republican Etiquette, and Guide to Correct Personal Habits, Embracing an Exposition of the Principles of Good Manners* (New York, 1887)

Willemsen, Annemarieke, 'Taking Up the Glove: Finds, Uses and Meanings of Gloves, Mittens and Gauntlets in Western Europe, *c.* AD 1300–1700', *Post-medieval Archaeology*, XLIX/1 (2015), pp. 1–36

Wood, Mrs Henry, *Mrs Halliburton's Troubles*, 20th edn (London, 1888)

PHOTO ACKNOWLEDGEMENTS

The author and publishers wish to express their thanks to the below sources of illustrative material and/or permission to reproduce it. Every effort has been made to contact copyright holders; should there be any we have been unable to reach or to whom inaccurate acknowledgements have been made please contact the publishers, and full adjustments will be made to any subsequent printings. Some locations of artworks are also given below, in the interest of brevity:

Alamy: pp. 18 (Danita Delimont), 130 (Heritage Image Partnership Ltd), 131 (ScreenProd/Photononstop), 136 (ScreenProd/Photononstop), 140 (Zechina); The Museum of the American Printing House for the Blind, Louisville, KT: p. 88; Amsterdam Museum, Amsterdam: p. 154; Art Properties, Avery Achitectural & Fine Arts Library, Columbia University, New York (C00.1483.300): p. 129; Baltimore Museum of Art, MD: p. 145; British Library, London (MS Harley 4380, fol. 141r): p. 91; Cleveland Museum of Art, OH: pp. 167, 184; Cornell University Library, Division of Rare and Manuscript Collections, Ithaca, NY: p. 91 (Susan H. Douglas Political Americana Collection, #2214); © DACS, 2021: p. 171; Dallas Museum of Art, TX: p. 44; © Coll. Musée dauphinois – Département de l'Isère: pp. 60, 71; Gemäldegalerie Alte Meister, Schloss Wilhelmshöhe, Kassel: p. 52; Getty Images: pp. 36 (De Agostini Picture Library), 92 (Angelo Cozzi/Archivio Angelo Cozzi/Mondadori), 199 (Larry Busacca), 200 (Noam Galai), 205 (Dave M. Benett); The J. Paul Getty Museum, Los Angeles: p. 151; from Denis Diderot and Jean-Baptiste le Rond d'Alembert, *Recueil de planches, sur les sciences, les arts libéraux, et les arts méchaniques, avec leur explication*, vol. III (Paris, 1765), photos courtesy Getty Research Institute, Los Angeles: pp. 46, 47; The Glove Collection Trust: pp. 26, 37, 40, 49, 82, 93, 179; photos Anne Green: pp. 57, 59, 102; Horniman Museum and Gardens: p. 133 (object no. nn3804); courtesy Hprints: p. 120; Huntington Library, San Marino, CA: p. 87; © KHM-Museumsverband, CC BY-NC-SA 4.0: p. 6; Los Angeles County Museum of Art (LACMA): p. 53; courtesy Shaun Leane: p. 207; Library of Congress, Prints and Photographs Division, Washington, DC: pp. 103 (photo Al Ravenna), 188; The Metropolitan Museum of Art, New York: pp. 30, 90, 98, 166; photo Hansel Mieth/The LIFE Picture Collection/Shutterstock: p. 81; © Morphy Auctions, Denver, PA: p. 67; Musée d'Orsay, Paris: p. 142; Museum of Fine Arts, Boston, MA: pp. 21, 112; NASA: pp. 195 (Bill Ingalls), 196 (Ulrich Lotzmann, Amanda Young and Bill Ayrey); National Gallery of Victoria, Melbourne: p. 109; Nordiska musset, Stockholm, CC BY-NC-ND (photo Mona-Lisa Djerf): p. 153; private collection/location unknown: p. 70; Carole Raddato, CC BY-SA 2.0: p. 15; Rama, CC BY-SA 2.0 FR: p. 20; Rijksmuseum, Amsterdam: pp. 56, 160; The Samuel Courtauld Trust, The Courtauld Gallery, London: p. 104; Shutterstock.com: pp. 78 (QiuJu Song), 128 (Hamza Ali Shatnawi), 132 (Victor Grow), 191 (Victor Moussa), 192 (Khairil Azhar Junos), 193 (ra3rn), 194 (Alin_Kris), 201 (Shaun Jeffers); Smithsonian Institution, Department of Anthropology: p. 118 (Catalog number E38455B/photo Donald E. Hurlbert); © 2009 Laura Splan: p. 203; Staatsbibliothek zu Berlin (Ms. Germ. fol. 623, 22v): p. 24; T-LABEL: p. 174 (photo Taylor-Bea Gordon); Victoria and Albert Museum, London: pp. 12, 17, 27, 66, 178, 181; Yale Center for British Art, Paul Mellon Collection, New Haven, CT: p. 96.

INDEX

Page numbers in *italics* indicate illustrations